"We wait with great expectation for God to use this book to mobilize the community of faith. Packed with advice, insight, and example, it calls us to a refreshing biblical approach to successful ministry. Tom White's vision is not wishful thinking!"

Joe Aldrich
President Emeritus,
Multnomah Bible College and Seminary

"Pastors' Prayer Summits, city-wide praise events, and concerts of prayer have all created an appetite for the glory of God among Christians. If your hope burns like hunger, then this book is for you. Here you'll find the story of how Tom and others have been proving out the biblical promises for transformation through slow-growht, practical wisdom."

Steve Hawthorne
Director, Waymakers

"Tom White is a true pioneer in cultivating the concept of a dynamic city-wide prayer movement. He has distilled his years of experience into this timely and remarkable book. It could well provide the blueprint for just such a movement in your community.

Dick Eastman
International President, Every Home for Christ

City-Wide Prayer Movements

One Church, Many Congregations

TOM WHITE

VINE
BOOKS

SERVANT PUBLICATIONS
ANN ARBOR, MICHIGAN

Vine Books is an imprint of Servant Publications especially designed to serve evangelical Christians.

Published by Servant Publications
P.O. Box 8617
Ann Arbor, Michigan 48107

Cover design by Uttley/DouPonce DesignWorks, Sisters, Oregon

01 02 03 04 10 9 8 7 6 5 4 3 2 1

Printed in the United States of America
ISBN 1-56955-242-8

Library of Congress Cataloging-in-Publication Data

White, Tom, 1947-
    City-wide prayer movements : one church, many congregations / Tom White.
        p. cm.
    Includes bibliographical references.
    ISBN 1-56955-242-8 (alk. paper)
     1. Evangelistic work. I. Title.
    BV3790 .W476 2001
    269' .2'0973—dc21

                                                                    2001003128

Dedication

For any lasting fruit that remains from this book, I am indebted to Dr. Joe Aldrich, President Emeritus of Multnomah Bible College and Seminary and founder of the Pastors Prayer Summit movement. "Dr. Joe's" undying passion for unity in the Body of Christ has inspired and undergirded my calling to pray and labor for tangible expressions of the John 17 witness of oneness that compels unbelieving skeptics to become saints.

Contents

Acknowledgements

Deepest and enduring thanks to three stalwart helpers who waded through my initial burst of verbosity, and brought better focus to my work:

Kathy Deering of Servant Publications, who managed the editorial substance of the project with a keen appreciation for its spirit; my wife Terri, who has ably colabored with me in this calling and who provided invaluable insight and input; and my son Josh White, whose discernment, writing skills, and leadership will one day far outshine my own.

And special thanks to Jerry and Sandra Kwast, local and long-time friends, who provide me an "upper room" country office where I regularly settle my spirit, collect my thoughts, and word-craft.

Foreword

In 1984, nearly 3,000 prayer leaders from 70 nations gathered in Seoul, Korea, for the first-ever International Prayer Assembly for World Evangelization (IPA). Sponsored by the Lausanne Committee and the World Evangelical Fellowship, our week together uncovered, to our utter amazement, many concerted prayer movements unfolding already in scores of nations. Even more arresting was that many of these movements centered on major cities. Clearly, God was up to something.

In the years since then, prayer movements have grown with leaps and bounds! I have observed first-hand throughout the 1990s the growth of a multiethnic, multidenominational prayer initiative here in metropolitan New York city, incorporating hundreds of churches, over one thousand pastors, and thousands of serious Christians. All share a common commitment to seek the transformation of the world's most influential city through an urban-sized Christ-awakening in answer to our persevering intercession. Such an aggressive vision is not unique to New York. It can be found in a multitude of other communities across America, and beyond.

We still have a way to go, however, for these movements to accomplish all God intends. Evangelical urbanologist Dr. Ray Bakke sets forth the need clearly. Out of nearly three hundred of his own urban consultations across the globe,

Bakke concluded that nine of the ten major barriers for reaching our cities for Christ are found *inside* the churches, not outside. Of those nine, he discovered, the greatest barrier is a *spirit of hopelessness.* In addition, Barna Research Associates recently observed about Christians in our nation: "The challenge to today's Church is not methodological. It is a challenge to resuscitate the spiritual passion and fervor of the nation's Christians." Without a doubt, city-wide prayer movements must increase, deepen and accelerate—now more than ever. Divine intervention, in answer to our cries, can effectively replace hopelessness with a fresh reality of Christ and his kingdom, resuscitating exhausted Christians.

Tom White is right in the center of this effort. He is both a "pioneer" and a "practitioner" in the world of prayer movements. What a great combination! I vividly remember my first meeting with Tom. It was years ago in a retreat for the National Prayer Committee in the Pacific Northwest. I could see the "fire" burning in his eyes; and yet as we conversed his gentle, loving, pastoral heart came shining through as well. I wanted to spend time with him, learn from him, and partner with him. Graciously, God has allowed all three things to happen repeatedly as we have served city and national prayer movements together.

Tom and I have embraced the same fundamental mandate. Here's how he expresses it in chapter 4: "To promote a fervent pursuit of God that attracts his favor and results in loving unity and a revival of the Body of Christ across denominational, ethnic, and cultural lines, such that out of the unity and frequent worshipful prayer will emerge God-breathed strategies that minister his grace and mercy to the city."

Tom tells us that in concerted prayer we become *"pursuers of Christ's presence."* This is the bottom line of every city prayer movement since the one described in Zechariah 8:20-22. As Zechariah records the call: "Come, let us go at once and seek the Lord. I myself am going" (v.20).

Through fascinating case studies, compelling insights into Kingdom strategies, personal reflections as a practitioner, and nine (count them!) Appendices containing a mosaic of practical helps for any prayer leader, Tom White challenges all of us to break with the status quo. He summons us to break through into God's very best for our communities. Listen to him in Chapter 6: "You have a choice: to stay with the safety and predictability of the status quo or to see where God is going and rise in faith to go there at any cost...I trust these pages will stir you to break through barriers of unbelief, and press into new ground."

This book has certainly done that for me!

In fact, Tom has driven me back to where it all started for me, when as a young pastor in a university town I found myself in the thick of a revolution. Armed troops were in the streets; students were being shot and killed and wounded; the paralysis of fear and confusion lurked everywhere. Out of that crucible a group of us spent six solid weeks praying through the book of Ephesians, verse by verse, hours upon hours, seeking God for a work in our city that might replicate the mighty revival in Ephesus (described in Acts 19).

I have never been the same since. Those weeks convinced me of three things: (1) Prayer could be a wonderful experience, especially when you're in it with others. (2) Praying for a whole city (and not just ourselves) was truly the heart of

God's vision. (3) I could never be satisfied with anything less than a thorough Christ-awakening that impacts every dimension of the life of the city, beginning with the Church.

Thank you, Tom, for revitalizing those convictions for me. Your writing has given me renewed determination and invaluable know-how. What a blessing you have been, and continue to be to me and to the Body of Christ everywhere. May this book find its way into many hands and hearts, dispelling the spirit of hopelessness and igniting a wave of passionate pursuers of Christ.

David Bryant
(Founder/President, Concerts of Prayer International
Chairman, America's National Prayer Committee)

A Script Rewritten

I've always been a fan of books, movies, or TV dramas that have anything to do with a "mission impossible" made possible when ordinary people are endowed with extraordinary faith and determination. Not the popular adventure film hyped by fantasy, special effects, and a corny story line, but real-deal life stories: common men and women overcoming adversity with lives that mean something and leave an enduring message.

Serving the kingdom of God seems to me like one of those "mission impossible" plots. Although our ultimate destination is of course assured, we sign on, start walking by faith, and get our cues and maps as we go. When I started my spiritual journey in October, 1969, I had some initial inklings about what my life script might be, but the Master Playwright has surprised me many times with rewrites that leave my natural mind spinning.

In 1981, I was serving as the administrator of a multiple staff church in Corvallis, Oregon. Like a spring bubbling up out of rocky soil, there was in those days a fresh stirring in the hearts of some local pastors to pray together, to embrace repentance, and to cry out to God for revival. We weren't numerous, but we were honest and earnest. On occasion, some women intercessors prayed for and with us. During these early years, we took initiative to invite a few national prayer leaders to Corvallis to instruct and challenge us. We found ourselves increasingly captured by "stirrings" of the Spirit. At the time, this new journey felt a bit like stumbling in the dark with a key-ring flashlight and a map drawn in light pencil! But it somehow seemed clear that Jesus wanted to make his glory known in a special way in our city. I now look back on those days as a distinct season of faithful, persevering "intercessory investment."

By 1990, my script took on a new twist as, on occasion, something new began to happen in me on my living room floor or in a corner of a church at early morning prayer. I began crying out, sometimes with words, other times in speechless travail, for a Body-wide spiritual awakening.

Pioneers find themselves going places and doing things they do not pre-plan. Today many of us are familiar with such things as prayerwalking, prophetic prayer actions, prayers of birthing and travail, lighthouses of prayer, and intercessory prayer warfare. In the mid-1980s, such prayer applications were widely unfamiliar.

One cold, misty Easter morning eighteen or twenty prayer warriors from different churches piled into vans, plugged in worship tapes, and drove up Mary's Peak, the highest mountain in Oregon's coastal range, to proclaim the praises of God over our valley and its towns in an effort to weaken the grip of enemy strongholds. We had documentation that the peak was a prime site for witchcraft. Police reports revealed rampant vandalism and hate graffiti there. As we were driving down Main Street in Philomath, Corvallis' neighbor city to the west, I felt just a little bit nuts. No, I felt a *lot* nuts! "Lord, what am I doing, dragging this bunch out to stand in the cold rain, sing songs, and pray?"

At the summit, standing atop a gray concrete weather station in a cold drizzle, my doubts diminished. With "Our God Reigns" on our lips, the spiritual heavens opened, and the presence of God settled in over our goofy little band of Gideon warriors. Mostly we sang hymns and choruses extolling the Lord's goodness and sovereignty. Huddled under umbrellas (standard outdoor prayer gear in Oregon), we proclaimed Scripture. We lifted up Jesus' name in praise and worship. We exposed strongholds of darkness— intellectualism, pride, self-sufficiency, idolatry, witchcraft— and asked God to diminish their power over our land. This was far more about lifting up the Lord's name and standing on his promises than it was shouting at the devil. That day, the towns of the Willamette Valley were my "Jerusalem": "As the mountains surround Jerusalem, so the Lord surrounds his people both now and forevermore. The scepter of the wicked will not remain over the land allotted to the righteous" (Ps 125:2-3). We came away from that morning inspired and fired to press on further in strategic prayer for our area.

We wanted to grow in the art of praying "on site with insight."[1] Within a few weeks, our Corvallis pastors prayerwalked from the four compass points, meeting in the gazebo in Central Park for corporate prayer and debriefing. On another day, a crisp October morning, we prayerwalked the streets of our city's core, praying over businesses, buildings, and the Benton County Courthouse. I led a team on a sweep down Second Street, the locale of two New Age bookstores, curio shops, and an infamous local tavern. On Halloween Eve of 1986, we held a special gathering of saints called "Lifting up the Lord of Light," which included celebrative praise and worship, a bit of teaching on the historical roots of Halloween, some biblical injunctions on resisting evil, and corporate intercession for our city.

These prayer actions were all a part of the "intercessory investment," offering the Lord an initial down payment of faithful prayer on behalf of his work in our region. Any long-term spiritual result flows out of someone's sacrificial investment, a willingness to pour significant time, energy, and resource into a noble goal.

Having ministered for years in spiritual warfare, I had learned how God sets individuals and families free from bondage. I began to wonder, *can a city be "delivered" and brought into new levels of liberty in the power of God?* I was undergoing a personal change, from being a warrior always looking to advance the kingdom militantly, to being first a worshiper, enthralled with the beauty of the Lord's character. I became increasingly enamored with his *ways* and less concerned about trying to help him out with his *work.* I also came to recognize that though my heart motive was right, I was, in Solomon's words, "leaning on [my] own understanding." I needed to lean into God alone and learn the language of his Holy Spirit so I could increasingly speak and minister "in the mind of Christ." This core discipline has become the center of my interior life, serving as a gyrocompass that guides my outward endeavors. Since this is so central, I will explore it in depth in chapter 1.

By the late 1980s, something else was brewing in the Pacific Northwest. Up the road from me in Portland, Dr. Joe Aldrich, President of Multnomah Bible College, was wrestling with a question similar to my own: "What would it take to see a significant move of the Spirit of God initiated and sustained in a specific geographical community, resulting in unity in the Body of Christ, widespread evangelization of the lost, and measurable change in society?"[2] In chapter 2, I want to share about the founding of the Pastors Prayer Summit movement and how it began to impact my life in a profound way. After ten years of Prayer Summits, my life has been dramatically changed. Many of the illustrations in this book are a spillover from this crucible of personal and corporate transformation.

Also in chapter 2 I'll begin to explore the inspiration for building city-wide prayer movements. Chapter 3 unwraps the biblical blueprints and presents a rationale for the re-emergence of the "city church." Chapter 4 explains what leadership of a city-wide "house of the Lord" begins to look like. Chapters 5 and 6 get us right into the trenches with a realistic look at the hard work of maintaining healthy relationships and dealing with spiritual warfare issues. Chapter 7 shares both the "inspiration" for united, fervent prayer in the city environment, and the "perspiration" of various prayer activities that begin to emerge. In Chapter 8, I bring you up to date on "the rest of the story" from Oregon, and reflect on the future of spiritual renewal in cities and regions.

I'm a mix of pioneer and practitioner, dependent on the Lord for any lasting results. This book is not just another heap of unproven theory. It's not overly theological. But my earnest prayer is that what I have learned will be helpful to you both personally and as a member of the larger Body of Christ.

Already some are asking, "Is this city church model actually working anywhere? Are there any success stories?" There is a multitude of promising "works in progress." City-wide prayer movements seem to be making a long-term, sustainable investment in biblical unity, intercession, acts of mercy, and collaborative outreach that can bring maximum kingdom impact to a community.

In cities that have started down this road, we're seeing these kinds of results: (1) a deepening trust between leaders, (2) an increase of the health and growth of congregations, (3) more accountability for disgruntled or wounded sheep who move from church to church, (4) inter-church cooperation, (5) the ability to respond with one voice to local issues and crises, and (6) a shared ownership of a vision to impact the city. Such measurable, sustainable gains make embarking on this journey worthwhile.

God the Father wants to answer the impassioned prayer of his Son for those who follow him: "...that all of them may be one, Father, just as you are in me and I am in you ... so that the world may believe that you have sent me ... May they be brought to complete unity to let the world know that you sent me and have loved them even as you have loved me" (Jn 17:21-23). We wonder, do we not, whether this can ever be a reality? We dream about the Body of Jesus working as it is supposed to work somewhere, somehow. This book is about the spirit of Jesus' prayer springing up in hearts all across the world through what I am calling "city-wide prayer movements." There are many significant signs and streams of spiritual renewal happening in our time. The longing for answers to the John 17 prayer in city and regional environments is one of those streams, and this stream of hope is increasing in both strength and speed.

If you long to see the resurrection power of the Lord Jesus Christ permeate every level of your daily life and change the social fabric of the cities and counties you call home, I believe these pages will stir embers of faith planted deep in your soul and ignite a fire of vision for what our Lord can do if we simply make ourselves available to be an answer to his prayer.

Chapter 1

My Heart, His Home

Today the heart of God is an open wound of love. He aches over our distance and preoccupation. He mourns that we do not draw near to him. He grieves that we have forgotten him. He weeps over our obsession with much-ness and manyness. He longs for our presence. And he is inviting you—and me—to come home to where we belong, to come home to that for which we were created.

Richard Foster
Prayer: Finding the Heart's True Home

I was road weary, on another "East Coast swing" for several ministry assignments. It was late February, 1999, and I was on the shores of Canandaigua Lake in the Finger Lakes region of New York for a second Prayer Summit with leaders from many denominations. We had a relatively good second day, seeking God and sharing our burdens with each other.

That evening, we began with a mix of a cappella hymns and choruses, interspersed with sincere, earnest prayers. It just felt, well, predictable.

I like the word from James, "You do not have, because you do not ask God" (4:2). So I began to silently cry out in my spirit, "Lord, there's so little of your life and power in our singing, would you break into our midst and draw us to yourself?"

No more than two or three minutes later, a woman who had been silent the first day and a half led out with a personal love song to Jesus, with her own melody, in her own words. Suddenly, serenely, everything changed. One moment, we were a motley bunch trying to connect with God, fumbling and bumbling, doing the best we knew to do; the next moment a heavenly presence was filling the room. It was as if God had poured spiritual gasoline on the flame of adoring love lit in this sister's heart. One after another joined in, lifting voices in blended harmonies and melodies, expressing love for the Lord. To quote a grand old hymn, "Heaven came down and glory filled my soul!"

My Heart an Altar

In this book, we're looking at where and how the Lord is moving in our day to establish dwelling places of his presence among his people. My aim is to give you some of the "why" and the "how" related to the birthing and building of city-wide movements of prayer. We'll get to the details. But we must begin, and linger a bit, with the priority of personal devotion.

Here's my chief concern: what do you and I love more, the fulfilling fruit of kingdom expansion, or the King himself? Can you be so enamored with the beauty of the Lord that it outshines the latest "kingdom thing" that is flourishing (or failing) in your life?

Something Jesus said to his friends in the upper room has always left me unsettled. Sharing that he is the vine, and his disciples the branches, he says, "...apart from me you can do nothing" (Jn 15:5). He is speaking about bearing spiritual fruit, producing something that will last. We can be about many things and can appear to be on track. But is Jesus really in it? Is the sap of his vine flowing into my branch? Am I truly abiding, receiving, and releasing his life to others?

At the time of this writing, the church in America has seen much expenditure of time, energy, and resources in conferences and various methodologies hoping to usher in a widespread awakening. So far, except for some isolated bright spots, our leaders and lay folks are exhausted keeping pace with both the demands of our obsessive culture and an overly programmatic approach in our churches. There is a vast difference between programs that leave us spent and the presence of God that energizes holy obedience.

If we're not careful, we can fall prey to revival-expectation fatigue and its dreaded symptoms: spiritual disillusionment, cynicism, and unbelief, forgetting to heed Jesus' word to the believers at Ephesus to repent and return to him as first love (Rv 2:4-5) and to the Laodicean church to admit the emptiness of its pride and self-sufficiency. (Rv 3:17-18).

It is imperative that we pursue the Shepherd of our souls, wait before we work, and receive before we give. We must return again and again to this truth on four levels: (1) in our individual devotional lives, (2) in our homes, (3) in our church and home fellowships, and (4) in the wider city or regional expression of the Body of Christ. The spiritual depth of our own lives determines the quality of our family and church life. Only healthy church fellowships growing in God can contribute to a vibrant city-wide prayer movement.

Looking for longing hearts. Asa, King of Judah, began well but finished poorly (see 2 Chr 14–16). In his early years, he called the people back to seeking the Lord, initiated reforms, and exposed idolatry. He was on the right track. But this great man of God shows us a painful lesson. In his latter years, he faced a military insurgence from Baasha, King of Israel. He should have simply inquired of the Lord on how to respond, just as Jehoshaphat did years later in a far worse jam (2 Chr 20:12). However, even having known the ways of the Lord, Asa surprisingly fell into the ways of Saul, relying on his own wisdom. He sought an alliance with the King of Aram. Initially, it appeared that his scheme had worked, until the Spirit spoke through Hanani the seer. He rebuked the king for his refusal to bring the situation to God in the first place, and he shared these words, recorded for all peoples of all times to ponder: "For the eyes of the Lord range throughout the earth to strengthen those whose hearts are fully committed to him. You have done a foolish thing, and from now on you will be at war" (2 Chr 16:9).

Asa threw poor Hanani into jail, oppressed some local innocents, contracted a dreaded foot disease, and died, unrepentant. Any of us could slip into the same backslidden mess. Here's the nugget in this story: *the Lord is on a search for hearts yielded to him, and is waiting to strengthen, help, and empower those who have learned to seek him first before stepping off the curb and into the traffic.* It takes years for us to grow up into this. We need to keep seeking God for his own sake, then watch for *his* initiatives and leadings. I believe that this was the dynamic in the early days of the church; those first Christians were devoted to good teaching, deep relationships, confession at the Lord's table, and regular prayer. God did the rest: "Everyone was filled with awe, and many wonders and miraculous signs were done by the apostles" (Acts 2:43).

Evelyn Underhill has captured well the essence of what I am trying to say:

Adoration, and not intercession or petition, must be the very heart of the life of prayer. Prayer ... must begin, end, and be enclosed in the atmosphere of adoration, aiming at God for and in Himself. *Our ultimate effect as transmitters of the supernatural light and love depends on this adoring attentiveness.* In such a prayer of adoring attentiveness, we open our doors wide to receive His ever-present Spirit.

But sometimes we are in such a hurry to transmit, that we forget our primary duty is to receive; and that God's self-imparting through us will be in direct proportion to our adoring love and humble receptiveness. *Only when our souls are filled to the brim, can we presume to offer spiritual gifts to others.*

When we find that the demands made upon us are seriously threatening our inward poise, when we feel symptoms of starvation and stress, we can be quite sure that it is time to call a halt; to re-establish the fundamental relation of our souls with Eternal Reality, the home and Father of our spirits ... *It is only when our hearts are thus actually at rest in God, in peaceful and self-oblivious adoration, that we can hope to show His attractiveness to others* (emphases mine).[1]

Do *you* need to slow the pace of your life and adjust your priorities? I wrestle with this tension nearly every day. I dread the thought of being a King Asa, starting strong and ending with a sputter. Is my heart really "at rest" in God? Do I know what it is to regularly enter into "peaceful and self-oblivious adoration" of the Most High? Is my spiritual life attractive to others? If I cannot honestly grapple with these questions, and persevere in the search for answers, I have no business thinking that God is going to bring a revival to my town.

God gets excited about our excitement about him. As parents, our hearts leap in those rare moments when a child shares appreciation for who we are. On my fiftieth birthday, my daughter Melissa made a card, "Fifty Things That Make Dad Distinctive." Her powers of observation were scary! Some of the distinctives were downright embarrassing, revealing a few of my more extreme personality traits. But as I read the card, my father's heart was touched in a new way. *My child really knew me,* had studied my ways, had captured my flaws— yet she loved me! With forethought, Melissa had taken time to tell me, "Dad, I love you ... you've marked my life in a major way."

Our heavenly Father has a tender heart that longs for appreciation for who he is and what he does. And *his* character is flawless. I have come to believe that in all we say and do in our personal lives, our church communities, our vocational callings, our vacations, our seasons of sorrow and of joy—we are to be a people consumed with a passion to give God praise and pre-eminence in all things.

Whatever our calling and circumstances, we all need to learn to soak in God's revitalizing presence in the face of things that distract us and drain our energy.

One winter morning I turned on the kitchen light, and noticed that Terri had posted a little sign on a tiny shelf to the right of the sink:

Make a nest where your heart can rest.

This simple thought, "make a nest," captured me. Lord, my real home, my dwelling place, my only place of real peace and security, is near your altar.

How lovely is your dwelling place, O Lord Almighty! My soul yearns, even faints for the courts of the Lord; my heart and my flesh cry out for the living God. Even the sparrow has found a home, and the swallow a nest for herself, where she may have her young—a place near your altar, O Lord Almighty, my King and my God. Blessed are those who dwell in your house; they are ever praising you. Blessed are those whose strength is in you, who have set their hearts on pilgrimage.

PSALM 84:1-5

Making a nest where our hearts find rest can happen throughout the day, in any situation. We must learn to set up our own portable "tent of meeting" right in the midst of the normal flow of our lives. Sometimes, however, we have retreat settings that help our spiritual nesting.

A Nest Where Your Heart Can Rest

We were deep in the woods north of St. Petersburg, Russia, near the Finland border, in an encampment built by Russian intelligence during World War II. It was late September, and the cold breezes were violently twisting stands of white birches and scattering golden leaves. About one hundred servants of God, a mix of missionaries and Russian pastors, were meeting for a second Prayer Summit in 1996. We jammed into a room designed for recreational dancing, with gaudy pictures covering the walls. We came seeking refuge and fresh strength in the Lord.

To the locals, St. Petersburg is known as the "city of bones." Tsar Nicholas conscripted peasants to build the city, and thousands had died. He left their bodies to rot, and their bones were built into the foundation of the city. During World War II, German forces laid siege to the city over a two-year period, and the Russians held the line only at a great cost of life. That is why St. Petersburg, although a city of intellectual and cultural accomplishment, is known as a "city of death."

Gathering with these kingdom servants, I felt the shrouds of death hovering about like spirits of oppression and despair. The Summit had begun well with singing and sincere prayers. But as we moved to pray for one another the second day, a heaviness hung over the group. I shared with my co-facilitators, "I think we just need to let people pour out their hearts to God." The next hours were agonizing as the participants shared their discouragement, perplexities, and feelings of fruitlessness.

After our evening fare of Russian borscht, black bread, and

scrawny chicken (during which my mind wandered to my cache of peanuts and chocolate bars in my room), we regathered in the dance hall. Someone read Habakkuk 3, in which the prophet proclaims that though there are no figs, no grapes, no olives, no sheep, no cattle—nothing, nada, nyet—"yet I will rejoice in the Lord, I will be joyful in God my Savior" (3:18). I was humbled.

Another veteran missionary began to pray. The Holy Spirit quickened this brother's desperately sincere words. He ended his prayer with something like this, "Jesus, I just want to sit at your feet, and be with you." The group responded with song after song: "My Jesus, I love Thee, I know Thou art mine"; "As the deer pants for the waters, so my soul longs after Thee"; "I Love You, Lord, and I lift my voice to worship you." It was as if Jesus stepped into that room, calming fears and drying tears. Seasons of stillness, some of them ten to fifteen minutes, settled in over us. People's prayers turned noticeably more quiet and personal. "Jesus, thank you for giving me new hope tonight." "Lord, forgive my unbelief." "Father, it is enough just knowing you love me." These folk were not necessarily getting answers to all their questions, but they were getting answers to prayers for a supernatural peace that alone could guard their minds and hearts. They were making a nest where their troubled hearts could rest. I'll never forget that night in a dingy dance hall in the middle of a Russian nowhere when God heard the desperate cries of his people, and came near.

Setting my Heart on God Alone

If this kind of deepening of our devotional life is to happen, we have to make more room intentionally for the presence of God in our daily lives. A.W. Tozer wrote, "Complacency is a deadly foe of all religious growth. *Acute desire must be present or there will be no manifestation of Christ to his people. He waits to be wanted.*"[2] Two Old Testament figures, a king and a prophet, offer us striking models of this pursuit.

David, Shepherd Boy and King

David's psalms serve as a biblical "magna carta" for the pursuit of divine presence. He practiced this pursuit in the midst of horrific pain and perplexity, while being hunted as an enemy of the state. After his heart had been blinded by his sin with Bathsheba and the murder of her husband, he nevertheless was responsive to the word from Nathan, was open about his failure (Psalms 32 and 51), and made his way back into favor with his God. To his dying day, David was consumed with a love for Yahweh. The following portion of Psalm 27 captures this passion: "One thing I ask of the Lord, this is what I seek: that I may dwell in the house of the Lord all the days of my life, to gaze upon the beauty of the Lord and to seek him in his temple" (Ps 27:4). Shouldn't this be *our* passion and posture as well?

We have such a tendency to idealize biblical figures, as if they were inherently more spiritual than us moderns. They weren't. David battled his own distractions and personal foibles. His failures are recorded for all to see. Some of his outward circumstances were as bad as it gets. Inwardly, he must have suffered the pains of remorse and rejection. But notice in verse eight that David's inner man takes the initiative to instruct his soul, his outer man, "Your face, Lord, I will seek." This honest pursuer of peace with God learned to practice the vital discipline of collecting his inner self and calling his flawed outer self to give attention to staying in God's presence.

Jeremiah, the Pained Prophet

I have never faced anything close to what this weeping prophet endured. Although the message of the Lord burned in and through him with intensity and urgency, no one wanted to hear it. He was rejected and abused, and he wrestled regularly with chronic "why" questions. Yet he came to know the ways of God.

Here was a kingdom servant, caught between the glories of heaven and the hellishness of earth. On the one hand, "The Lord is with me like a mighty warrior ... Sing to the Lord! Give praise to the Lord!" (Jer 20:11, 13). But then we read verses 14 and 18: "Cursed be the day I was born ... Why did I ever come out of the womb to see trouble and sorrow and to end my days in shame?"

He is a good model for us because of the discrepancy between the prophetic stirrings that go on *inside* of us, and the hard realities we have to deal with on the *outside*. Has not God said this or that? Yes, but isn't the church in our city in a sorry state, with no one giving heed to what the Lord wants to do? Yes, often. And so we learn to persevere, as Jeremiah did, learning the deep lessons, waiting for God to work in his way, in his time.

Jeremiah's words become our bedrock:

This is what the Lord says: "Let not the wise man boast of his wisdom or the strong man boast of his strength or the rich man boast of his riches, but let him who boasts boast about this: that he understands and knows me, that I am the Lord, who exercises kindness, justice and righteousness on earth, for in these I delight," declares the Lord.

JEREMIAH 9:23, 24

Because of the deceitfulness of our own hearts—our pride, self-reliance, and vainglory—we must keep coming back to boasting only about knowing God and going where he is going. Anything devised by human ingenuity will lead us up cul-de-sacs.

Jeremiah had to deal with the wrenching pain of watching his people suffer under God's judgment. Having voiced his honest complaint, he affirms the all-sufficiency of the Lord's faithfulness:

Yet this I call to mind and therefore I have hope: Because of the Lord's great love we are not consumed, for his compassions never fail. They are new every morning; great is your faithfulness. I say to myself, "The Lord is my portion; therefore I will wait for him." The Lord is good to those whose hope is in him, to the one who seeks him; it is good to wait quietly for the salvation of the Lord.

LAMENTATIONS 3:21-26

"I say to myself, the Lord is my portion." Who's talking to whom? Jeremiah's spirit is talking to his soul. Anchored in eternal reality, his spiritual man is informing his outer man (mind and emotions) how to view his circumstances. No wonder Jeremiah can get to the real bottom line, "Let us examine our ways and test them, and let us return to the Lord" (3:40). May this be our passion and perspective. To be truly effective and fruitful ministering God's grace to others, we must first seek to receive the life of Christ in increasing measure.

Renewing Our Pursuing

As individual men and women we are fully responsible for the level of passion in our own hearts to pursue God. We can choose to seek him—or stay wherever we are. We can choose to call out for a greater enabling grace—or complain. We can choose, as Jeremiah did, to grow better in the face of disappointment—not bitter.

You may be an intercessor or a prayer warrior, stirred deeply as you read and reflect on these pages. You may be a pastor, seeking to understand how to increase an appetite for prayer and unity in your church. You may be holding down a 40-hour-a-week job, but feeling unfulfilled and sensing a call to be involved more in kingdom work. The quest for a wider spiritual awakening begins in the closet of your own heart.

Before reading on, I want to challenge you to take a few moments to work through the following exercise, asking the Father, the Son, and the Spirit to fan afresh in your heart the flame of "adoring attentiveness."

Setting My Heart to Seek

One thing I ask of the Lord, this is what I seek: That I may dwell in the house of the Lord all the days of my life, to gaze upon the beauty of the Lord and to seek him in his temple ... Hear my voice when I call, O Lord; be merciful to me and answer me. My heart says of you, "Seek his face!" Your face, Lord, I will seek.

PSALM 27:4, 7, 8

1. Read through the passage. Pause, pray, and ask the Lord to stir within you an increased desire to seek him. Read through the passage again, slowly, reflectively.

2. Has your spiritual fervor become lukewarm? If so, take a few moments and confess that you have drifted from your first love. Repent, receive his forgiveness, and return to a fresh resolve, "I will seek!"

3. If you were to identify the "one thing" of *your own heart,* how would you phrase it? Take a few moments to write your own psalm of devotion.

4. Close your time by praying or singing the personal psalm you've just written.

Chapter 2

A Call to the Construction Site

As you come to him, the living Stone—rejected by men but chosen by God and precious to him—you also, like living stones, are being built into a spiritual house.

1 PETER 2:4, 5a

Someday, church historians will point back to the 1990s as a decade of rising passion for worship and intercessory prayer in the worldwide Body of Christ. In many ways, it has also been a time for "assembling blueprints" and preparing for a new season of construction in the kingdom of God.

In the Preface, I mentioned Dr. Joe Aldrich, President of Multnomah Bible College in Portland, Oregon, who in 1989 was burdened by disunity in the Body of Christ. Here, stated again, was his question: "What would it take to see a significant move of the Spirit of God initiated and sustained in a specific geographical community, resulting in unity in the Body of Christ, widespread evangelization of the lost, and measurable change in society?" With a mix of desperation and humility, "Dr. Joe" called the spiritual leaders of Salem, Oregon together in February, 1989, to seek the Lord, with no set schedule and no special speaker.

This format of leaders sitting at Jesus' feet without an agenda spread quickly to numerous other cities, predominantly in the Pacific Northwest. He called it a "Prayer Summit," which began to be defined as:

> a prolonged (typically four-day) life-changing worship experience attended by a diversity of Christian leaders from specific, geographical communities whose sole purpose is to seek God, his kingdom, and his righteousness with the expectation that he will create and guide them through a humbling, healing, uniting process that will lead them to a unity of heart, mind, and mission and will qualify them for the blessing of God.[1]

The Church of the Valley

At a backwoods retreat center in the Puget Sound, my perspectives on kingdom building were retooled as I watched the Spirit of God bring leaders from all over the theological and ecclesiastical map into genuine brokenness over their sin. God called leaders to seek first *his* kingdom, and to cease from building empires that served only to energize human egos.

I returned to Corvallis with a passion to pursue this model in my own area. Getting a green light from Dr. Joe and his associate Terry Dirks, I called the pastors from the mid-Willamette Valley of Oregon to the first Prayer Summit in February, 1991. Taking a rookie's shot at facilitating the Summit, I found myself floundering, trying my best to follow the Holy Spirit. The muck and yuck of years of unresolved offenses, competition, and noncooperation between the pastors and churches of our area were dredged up. It was messy. At points I asked myself, "White—did you really hear God on this? Are you in your right mind believing there can be unity in the midst of so much mistrust and theological diversity?"

By Summit's end, we all felt we had been party to a divine meddling of miraculous proportion. God was clearly calling us to build something altogether new. In February 1992, at a second Summit attended by forty-two leaders, the "Church of the Valley" was born, a regional movement of prayer and worship in western Oregon.

There was a simple marvel in what was happening: we all fell in love in greater measure with God himself, and we began caring for one another at a whole new level. It just didn't matter that one was an old style Baptist, another a flaming Pentecostal, another a Missouri Synod Lutheran, or another a fiery Hispanic pastor. Presbyterian, Nazarene, Foursquare, Episcopalian, high church, low church, big church, cell church, tongues aflame with the Spirit and tongues proclaiming the Word of God in plain English. We will always have "labels." It is part of the natural man thing. We interpret things differently, worship differently, and develop diverse emphases of ministry. We decided to simply let the Lord cover over our various labels with the banner of his holy love.

A year later the pastors of the Church of the Valley met again. In the evening, our facilitator shared an illustration from an American Western. You know the classic showdown— the tough hombres ride into town, dismount and swagger, staring down any who dare to look their way. Up steps the Marshal. The whole town is on edge, watching. "Drop your weapons, men." The voice of authority. Reluctantly, slowly, the outlaws comply, loosening their belts, and handing over their weapons.

"Brothers, what weapons are you carrying into this room tonight? Criticism, resentment, envy, spiritual pride that judges your brother as a theological heretic? The Spirit of God is saying tonight, 'Gentlemen, drop your weapons.'" After a hushed silence, men stepped up to the communion table and confessed their sins, in some cases wrong attitudes toward others in the room.

A Baptist pastor spoke from the shadows: "I've been sitting and watching this, thinking, 'Lord, my heart is right, I don't have any heavy iron hanging from my spiritual hip.' But brothers, I've got to be honest, there's a derringer in my boot—I've been critical of my charismatic brothers—I've judged your doctrine and your style of worship." With that, he crossed the room, embraced a charismatic pastor, and sought forgiveness. This simple act of obedience opened a floodgate of confession and cleansing that carried on into the night.

The "Church of the Valley" was not just another ecumenical organization. No, this was the "real deal," covenantal love as it was meant to be. *The simple power of humility and holy love is what will break and subdue the insidious power of the flesh and the devil, and open a door for the visitation of the Lord to a city.*

Since those formative days, time after time, city after city, in different cultural contexts, I have watched God the Father, Son, and Spirit work in the hearts of men and women, melting spiritual pride, stirring devotional passion, breaking down dividing walls of theological bias, reconciling estranged relationships, healing emotional wounds, restoring broken marriages, and releasing a new vision to walk and work together to make Jesus known to a city or region. I've been "hanging around" this construction site ever since!

Relational Love—the Foundation

I believe that an annual Prayer Summit or its equivalent, and frequency of prayer and worship throughout the year, is the foundation on which a city-wide prayer movement must be built.

Let me tell you why I feel this so strongly. You cannot build a sustainable city-reaching movement on cooperative projects, events, or occasional tactical endeavors. Cement needs to be well mixed, poured with care, and seasoned. Time is one of our most precious commodities. It takes time, in a nondistracting environment, to build trust in a relationship, to discover and appreciate one another, to share common meals, to agonize over our pains and problems, and to rejoice in God's goodness.

Being in the presence of God together is the touchstone of our journey, an altar of remembrance when God speaks or moves. We have to "get out of Dodge" to do this. Jesus disappeared regularly. He spent significant "down time" with his disciples. Where and when can we get real with our Lord and our peers, and ask for prayer? Where and when can we—

- find delight in one another that releases joy for our common journey in a church or city?
- feel the heart of God and hear his voice for our ministries and cities?
- let the Holy Spirit search the dark corners of our hearts and lead us to confession?
- hear God speak and download the burdens of his heart for our city or area?

God is waiting to pour blessing on a unity of relationships rooted in authentic love. Before we plunge headlong into plans and projects, will we give him the time and opportunity to first build a firm, enduring foundation?

Qualifying for Covenant Blessing

Psalm 133:1 proclaims, "How good and pleasant it is when brothers live together in unity!" Do we really believe such harmony is achievable, or is this a sentimental fantasy? Listen to the Apostle Paul: "May the God who gives endurance and encouragement give you a spirit of unity among yourselves as you follow Christ Jesus, so that with one heart and mouth you may glorify the God and Father of our Lord Jesus Christ" (Rom 15:5, 6).

Harmony among brothers and sisters in the family of faith attracts the Father's favor. A heart consecrated by brokenness and obedience attracts the anointing of heaven. Our getting along, our willingness to look past one another's foibles and flaws, qualifies us for his blessing.

David wasn't talking about faking our real feelings just to get along. That would be too easy, too common. "I think you're a jerk, but God says I'm supposed to like you, so sure, I like you just fine." This is about finding *delight* in one another, embracing *mutual endearment,* promoting the welfare and blessing of our neighbors. This is about God himself imparting supernatural grace to rise above our self-centeredness and really care for those different from ourselves. Can this work in the real world?

Marcel Rebiai, half Jew, half Arab, part Moroccan, part Swiss, leads "Communities of Reconciliation" in Switzerland,

France and Jerusalem.*   Marcel is a remarkable man who knows well how hard it is to love "irregular people." He knows the daily rigors of people getting on your nerves, people stuck in the dysfunction of family-of-origin issues, people with years of unresolved pain and bitterness. Marcel shares that Jesus calls us to a level of love that bears up, suffers long, believes the best, endures insult, and covers a multitude of sins. Christians like Marcel make me ashamed of the shallowness of our Americanized brand of "churchianity." May God grant us a more authentic experience of what it is to pay the price of living in covenantal relationship with him, and with one another.

Weak Foundations

In too many places, it would be hard for an objective observer to really believe that the local churches were a functional part of the same "family dwelling." Whether we're looking at a big city, a regional grouping of towns, or a rural environment, the house of the Lord has serious cracks in its foundation. Aren't you sometimes embarrassed by this? In all too many places, the best expression of Christian unity is a monthly ministerial luncheon—typically a mix of eating, social connection, some form of relevant input, with a minimum of prayer tacked on after dessert. Or, it may be an ecumenical service on Christmas Eve, Good Friday, or Pentecost Sunday. Is this anywhere close to what Paul was getting at with his exhortation to

*Singles, couples with children, young and old, live, eat, and work together. They look for creative ways to minister Jesus' compassion to the needs of the cultures where they dwell.

the believers in Ephesus? "Make every effort to keep the unity of the Spirit through the bond of peace. There is one body and one Spirit ... one Lord, one faith, one baptism; one God and Father of all, who is over all and through all and in all" (Eph 4:3-6).

Are you bothered by the lack of authentic spiritual connection between your local ministers and the levels of isolation and fragmentation that keep your churches laboring in their own backyards, separated by fences of theological pride and ministry style? Have you long ago given up on the whole mess, or are you stirred by the possibility that God may be changing the status quo?

A Desire to Dwell

Our Lord has always searched for a people or place in which to deposit his glory. He says to Israel, "I will look on you with favor and make you fruitful and increase your numbers, and I will keep my covenant with you ... I will put my dwelling place among you, and I will not abhor you. I will walk among you and be your God, and you will be my people" (Lv 26:9-12).

The essence of covenantal love oozes out of these words— an intense longing to impart favor and fullness of life. This is the upside. The downside is equally clear. Yahweh is a jealous God, desiring adoration and allegiance. The balance of Leviticus carries the qualifying "but" that puts this covenantal relationship squarely in the people's court. If you do your best to love and obey me, blessings. But if you spurn my love and go your own way, you will suffer the consequences. When

Moses came down from Sinai and explained this covenantal relationship with God, "The people all responded together, 'We will do everything the Lord has said" (Ex 19:8).

But the Maker of covenants knew his people would fall short. He knew that Israel could not be expected to measure up all the way, all the time. So, the loving loophole, in Leviticus 26:40-42 (my paraphrase): "when you blow it, humble your miserable, backslidden selves, confess your sins, and I'll restore you. I'll remember every word I said to Abraham and Isaac, and will maintain my faithfulness." In other words, from the start, God bends over backwards to keep connecting with those he loves.

How is it that we, limited to our physical senses and mortal minds, can connect with God, who is invisible? The Lord knows that apart from some tangible manifestation, everyday people grope at best when it comes to knowing how to talk and walk with a purely spiritual being who is "up" or "out" there. So God has given his people a succession of tangible places where they can be sure to find him—from the building of places of remembrance, to a tabernacle in the wilderness, to a physical temple, and now to a spiritual temple built with the "living stones" of redeemed people.

Touched by His Glory

Let me illustrate how this kind of connection can happen. In May, 2000, I was helping to facilitate a Prayer Summit in Adelaide, Australia. After a false start and some human fumbling, someone led out with the familiar chorus, "I Love You, Lord," followed by another song that fanned the flame of devotional love. We made the shift from singing songs we knew to singing in the Spirit, making melodies and harmonies in our hearts and with our lips that were woven together as a tapestry of praise (see Eph 5:19). Typically, after a crescendo of participation, the intensity of such singing tapers off and quiets down. But on this night, each tapering down was followed by another rising up, as if God himself were drawing nearer in successive waves of his presence. I found myself singing some of the Lord's names in Hebrew, "Adonai, Elohim, Hallejuia, Elohim," and singing, "Kadosh, Kadosh, Kadosh!" (Hebrew for "holy"). Across the circle, a Jewish-Christian intercessor began singing in Hebrew. I became aware that we were singing antiphonally, back and forth. In a manifest way, God was ministering personally to men and women who had intentionally set aside time to pursue him with all their hearts.

Spontaneous and sincere confessions began bubbling up, spilling into the room. This humble dining room of the Aldinga Bay Holiday Village on the coast of South Australia was transformed into a virtual "Tent of Meeting." The cloud of his glory had descended, enveloping his people. We had been graced with a special moment of meeting.

It's true that we cannot and dare not demand or expect that God will just "show up" at our whim. But we can become pursuers of his presence, sharing our deepest longings, and letting him choose the times and places where he unveils himself to us in increased measure. We can practice this holy pursuit in our own quiet times, at family prayer altars, in home studies and prayer meetings, or at church on a Sunday night. Let's look for opportunities to open doors for God's visitation.

Haggai: A Call to Return and Rebuild

I want to focus on a specific historical construction site, the rebuilding of Solomon's temple after the exile. Suffering the despair of displacement from their land, and laboring under an oppressive government, Israel needed a reminder that *when they give priority to God's heart and the building of his house, the curse can lift and blessing return.* Obedience to covenantal principles will always attract God's favor afresh.

The rebuilding of the Temple had commenced around 535, but had been delayed. Haggai began to prophesy around 522. He reminded his peers of the results of breaking covenant: all the energy and time you expend goes down the drain if you're not following God (1:6). This was already a painful, proven fact. It is likely that Haggai himself had been present to witness the horrific destruction of the temple (2:3), and carried the pain of that within him. He spoke straight: "Wake up, people! You're spending time pursuing your own comfort, doing your own thing, and forgetting who you are and what we're about as a people." God's prophet faithfully spoke the truth and the Holy Spirit riveted the word into the people's hearts.

Zerubbabel, the Governor, and Joshua, the Priest, "got it" and went with it. From the text it appears that when the leaders were bold enough to say, "This is God," the people caught it, and feared the Lord (1:12). So, here we are—seeing the revelation, and responding with holy fear and obedience—a right response (for a change). So what's next? A further prophetic revelation from the Father, "I am with you!"

Now look at Haggai 2:4: "'Be strong ... and work ... for I am with you,' declares the Lord." This is language very similar to the encouragement King David shared to stir his son Solomon to launch out and build the first temple.

And there are specific words calling Israel to guard against two timeless enemies: fear and discouragement. Count on it—whenever we're called onto the construction site to build God's house, both human and spiritual opposition will arise. *It is only by fixing our gaze on the clarity and certainty of the heavenly vision, and following the voice of his Spirit and the initiatives of his appointed leaders, that we break through barriers of unbelief.*

The Lord talks about filling "this present house" with a glory greater than that of the "former house" (2:9). This, I feel, is one of the most significant yet untouched portions of prophetic scripture. The glory is the power and radiance of his own presence, visiting the place where he desires to dwell with his people. And yet, says Yahweh, if you think that the glory is something to behold now, in this rebuilt temple, wait until my Son, your coming Messiah, steps into it! (see Mt 21:12-15). "In this place, I will grant peace" declares the Lord (2:9). A place where his presence is made available. A place that is for a season a building, but then becomes a person, the "I am" of Jesus Christ. Only Yeshua, the Lord of peace, can bring true shalom to men's hearts. The book of Hebrews is full of this revelation. Through offering his body and blood in the natural, Jesus entered into the "Most Holy Place" of the spiritual tabernacle, atoning once and for all for the sins of all peoples of all times (Heb 9:11-14). Thus, through Jesus' blood, believers may enter the Most Holy Place, drawing near to God, free to share communion with him (Heb 10:19-22). What an awesome reality! Access, immediately, freely, to the heart of the Father.

But the amazing truth is that the place of access to God is within, not without. Paul writes, "Don't you know that you yourselves are God's temple and that God's Spirit lives in you?" (1 Cor 3:16). So, just as the temple in Jerusalem needed to be rebuilt, we need a restored vision of how God is building a house for his habitation in our day.

The House of The Lord

So, we ourselves are temples of the living God. We no longer need to be Jewish. We no longer need stone, mortar, fine wood, tapestries, and gold. He has promised to pour his presence into jars of human clay.

Paul's "Holy Temple"

You may have done a walk-through on a construction site, inspecting the fresh studs in place, the wiring and plumbing in view, the insulation stacked and ready. I love to peer at the blueprints, then walk through each room, smelling the fresh-cut wood and imagining what the finished product will be like.

As nice as it is to look at and appreciate, however, a new building is not a home until its occupants settle in.

Paul describes in Ephesians 2 a "holy temple in the Lord," a place intended for God's habitation, a place where both Jew and Gentile are welcome. The Gentiles, once "far away," are now drawn near and invited into the Father's "forever family room." No one but Yahweh, Creator and Lover of all souls, can bring Jews and Arabs, Asians and Americans, Brazilians and Buddhists, atheists and animists, billionaires and bums, into one room, with one essential identity, and with the same purpose. Only Jesus can conquer our sins of pride and racial superiority, and call us to be "one new man" (2:15). There is no other blueprint available and no other way to make the house a home.

For too long we have justified divisions between people of varying cultural and religious backgrounds. We face a range of doctrinal distinctives that all too often divide one believer from another. We major so much on having the right doctrines, the right forms of church government, and preferred styles of worship, that we minor on being obedient to the core of Jesus' exhortations to lay aside our bickerings and love one another from the heart. Can we start to pay attention and allow God to lay out the blueprints of his "holy temple," the dwelling place of his Spirit?

Peter's "Living Stones"

Whereas Paul provides a theological treatise on the new form of the church, Peter's language is more vivid. Those who trust in Jesus are "living stones ... being built into a spiritual house to be a holy priesthood" (1 Pt 2:5). This is an old covenant priestly commission baptized with fresh oil. God seeks closeness, relational proximity. He wants his chosen brought near through the blood of his Son, and empowered to declare his praises to the peoples and nations of the earth (2:9).

Acts offers a wealth of corroborative evidences. Look at how Luke described the emerging church in Jerusalem: "All the believers were one in heart and mind" (4:32a). When the word began spreading, "the number of disciples *in* Jerusalem increased rapidly" (6:7). "Great persecution broke out against *the church at Jerusalem*" (8:1). Luke describes divine activity occurring in "the church" (singular) throughout Judea, Galilee, and Samaria, saying that *it* was strengthened, and *it* grew in numbers (9:31). Obviously, in this emerging scenario, there was not yet time for personality differences and doctrinal issues to begin a process of fragmentation. We see this beginning to occur most overtly in Corinth. But does not this notion of the church of the city capture our Lord's original design and intent for one church expressed in diverse, but spiritually unified, congregations?

Paul's epistles to the believers residing in Ephesus, Colossae, and Philippi add further strength to the case. Take a look at one of these: "To all in Rome who are loved by God and called to be saints: grace and peace to you..." (Rom 1:7). Can the inherent oneness of the Body in a place be any more explicit? Paul appeals to the believers at Corinth, "I appeal ... that all of you agree with one another so that there may be no divisions among you and that you may be perfectly united in mind and thought" (1 Cor 1:10). In each epistle, he deals with specific issues that relate to their context and unique spiritual circumstances. It is evident to me that we have drifted far afield from the biblical norm of organic spiritual unity.

Everyone will surely not easily embrace the notion of the "city church." The very idea stretches the status quo. Some pastors and denominations just won't "go there." But I believe this is where Jesus' Body was at its emergence, and where it will be again as we approach the end of the current age.

What do non-Christians really "see" when they look at the church? How many places in this world provide a living model of a diverse assortment of miscellaneous "living stones" that are in process of being built into a spiritual mansion that is occupied by the King of the Universe?

Is the "City Church" a Biblical Concept?

By now, there may be some of you asking if this notion of "one church, many congregations" is found in the Scriptures, or if it is just another good idea.

In the formative years of the church, believers in various house churches regarded themselves as the "church of Antioch," or the "church of Berea." Over time there was the natural development of various groupings based on cultural affinities, leadership, worship styles, and theological distinctives. But when the apostle Paul framed his epistles, they were addressed generally to all the believers in the cities of Ephesus, Philippi, or Thessalonica. Amidst a diversity of congregations, we may surmise that there was a clear corporate identity of the people of God living in that particular place, serving the same Lord and filled with the same Spirit. So when Paul exhorts the believers in Ephesus to "make every effort to keep the unity of the Spirit through the bond of peace" (Eph 4:3), he is speaking to the one church of the city made up of diverse congregations.

It is also instructive that the last words from Jesus recorded in Scripture came in the form of letters dictated specifically to the corporate "churches" of seven cities in Asia Minor, to the "church in Smyrna ... to the church in Sardis," and so forth. Clearly, Jesus was wanting to share a word with all of his followers who resided in each of these places. There are specific commendations and exhortations for each unique, geographically defined expression of his body.

So through twenty centuries, we have succeeded in fragmenting into so many separate affinity groups that we lose count. Could it be that when our Lord looks at a city, he does not read our labels, but rather sees us collectively as the saints of that city bearing the same family name, committed to the same holy purpose?

Mission Spokane, a healthy, developing city-wide movement in Eastern Washington State (www.missionspokane.org). has written a "Brief Apologetic for the City Church," in which they identify one of the predominant strengths of the formative early church, specifically:

...the existence of a practical and relational unity of the people of God in any given city. We would propose that the absence of biblical city-wide unity by the church today has had a detrimental impact upon the life and witness of God's people in the city. Stated positively, we believe that the presence of a biblically united and healthy city-church results in God blessing his people with a level of church life and public witness otherwise absent in that city. We believe that God, in some important way, deals with his people on a city-wide basis.

Isn't this consistent with the explicit language of both Paul and Peter? I'm convinced that Jesus is wanting to impart to us a fresh grace to embrace our innate spiritual unity.

Francis Frangipane, in his groundbreaking 1991 classic *The House of the Lord* captures well Jesus' central passion: "While the redemption of many was always motivating Jesus, his most ardent desire was his zeal for his Father's house; he was consumed with it (Jn 2:17). Building the house of God, the born-again, praying, loving city-wide church is still Christ's highest priority."[2] This fresh grace may come during a season of prosperity, or it may take the pressure of a common crisis or adversity, as in New Testament times.

Back to the Blueprints

So what do the blueprints for God's dwelling place look like? What's taking shape on the construction sites? As men and women step past their fears of compromise and embrace Jesus' command to love, celebrating their unique distinctives and honoring one another's strengths, handling their differences with maturity, they find that God's plans are similar from place to place, and yet distinctive. Perhaps worship leaders from many different churches will meet monthly for breakfast to share their lives and their songs with one another. Perhaps Christians in a region will collaborate together on city-wide training events. Increasingly, in many places, the Body of Jesus is coming together to form a "house of prayer" to lift up intercession over the city and beyond.

Our Citichurch of Corvallis letterhead shows a picture of the

County Courthouse surrounded by different church buildings. Participating congregations contribute financially to support a part-time administrator, and to sustain LOVE, Inc. ("In the Name of Christ"), a city-wide cooperative endeavor to meet people's felt needs. People in our churches are available to serve the school district as reading tutors, lunch buddies for troubled kids, and facility maintenance. Some city movements have raised funds to place a Jesus video in every home, and mobilize people to prayerwalk the neighborhoods when they deliver them.

A Place to Dwell

In June, 1999, a video called *Transformations* was produced and released by researcher and author George Otis Jr. The film documents four cities on three continents that have been dramatically changed by the power of the Holy Spirit. Very often, at the conclusion of this video, those who have seen it explode with clapping, cheering, shouting, whistling, laughing, crying ... trying in some manner to express thanks to God for what he is doing, and to respond in hope that he just might want to do something equally profound in their region. A follow-up video, *Transformations II*, realeased in June 2001, documents regions, not just cities, where the Spirit of God is active in earthly dwelling places.

We know about times in the past when the Lord has "come to town" in places of his choosing. At Asbury College in 1971, he came, and "chapel wasn't over." In Wales, a simple man, Evan Roberts, prayed, "Lord, bend me," and the Holy Spirit was poured out over the land. As you read, reflect, and pray through these pages, may you allow that same Spirit to stir you with a holy craving for God to find a fresh dwelling place in your own heart. May he quicken a renewed fervor to invite him, in greater measure, to take up residence in your church fellowship. And may you be captured with the possibility that God can manifest his presence in your city, visiting not only one church or denomination, but all congregations, reviving saints, redeeming people of every age, kind and color, healing the sick, giving hope to the brokenhearted, and transforming society as we know it. This is not mere wishful thinking, but a genuine offer that springs from the Spirit who can do anything, anywhere.

God is calling us to a new understanding of how to "do church." For those with ears to hear, his Spirit is calling us to the construction site to build a place for him to inhabit. In the pages that follow, I will endeavor to describe what this building project looks like, and how to use some of the tools. As we lay out the blueprints, I'd like to challenge you to pray along three distinct lines:

1) Ask the Father to impart to you a simple desire to seek him just for who he is, to draw near to him, and to know him better. Remember, God is the original "connector." He is waiting and watching for you to come and sit at his feet and say, "Lord, I don't know how this is going to happen, but I want to go deeper in your presence."

2) Ask God the Father, the Son, and the Spirit to release to you, and to your city, town, or region, a revelation of the priority of building a "spiritual house" for his habitation. This must come from him. Ask him to raise up prophetic voices to speak it, pastors to crave

it, intercessors to cry out for it, and people to get desperate for it.

3) Ask God to raise up leaders of the churches in your town who will see what he is doing, embrace it without fear, and move forward by faith, seeing that they are responsible not only for shepherding their own congregations, but also for how seriously they take the role of shepherding the collective numbers of lost souls in their city.

Chapter 3

Laying Out the Blueprints

Unless the Lord builds the house, its builders labor in vain. Unless the Lord watches over the city, the watchmen stand guard in vain.

PSALM 127:1

The second law of thermodynamics tells us that everything in the physical order is moving toward deterioration—rotting, rusting, slowly falling apart. That's a fact fifty-somethings like me don't want to face. And yet, that which is of the Spirit is moving in the opposite direction. Paul speaks of this in 2 Corinthians 4:16: "We do not lose heart. Though outwardly we are wasting away, yet inwardly we are being renewed day by day."

The natural order will fade away. But whatever is birthed and sustained in the spiritual realm lasts forever. Our Lord has the blueprints that will help us work together to bring his kingdom to this tired earth, specifically, to our own backyards. With the gifts and callings of his Spirit, we can discern what he is doing and choose to work with the Master Craftsman.

Restoring the Ruins

Israel endured an agonizing exile in Babylon. In 538 B.C., God intervened in a dramatic manner. He moved on the heart of Cyrus, king of Babylon, and placed a mantle of leadership on some men to restore the ruins of Solomon's temple. The books of Ezra, Nehemiah, Haggai, and Zechariah provide us with an astounding account of God's personal project to restore the temple and the worship of his name. Over two generations these and others carefully followed his ways in restoring the place of his dwelling, and the protective wall around it. Haggai and Zechariah (prophets), Zerubbabel (governor of Judah), Ezra (priest), and Nehemiah (apostolic builder) serve as prototypical models of spiritual reform. We would be wise to learn from these worthy mentors.

The Time Line: Rubble to Restoration

To set our context, here's what happened, and when:

538   Stirred by the Spirit of God, Cyrus decrees the return of the exiles to Jerusalem to rebuild the temple. Zerubbabel and some fifty thousand exiles begin the trek back home.

536   The foundation of the temple is completed, and opposition to the project begins to impede progress.

522   Under inspiration of the Spirit, Darius, King of Babylon, issues a decree to continue the temple project, and offers assistance with materials and labor.

520   The prophetic voices of Haggai and Zechariah stir the hearts of the leaders and the people to rise, build, and return to the Lord.

516   The work on the temple is completed.

460   Ezra and Nehemiah come under God's anointing to Jerusalem to oversee the rebuilding of the temple walls.

Over eighty years we see the acceleration of God's purpose to restore the broken connections with his people. When the Lord is truly in something, it unfolds with a rapidity that surprises even the hopeful. I want us to take a look at some biblical blueprints and patterns for reconnecting with God's presence, and the implications this might offer for the place where you live and minister.

Listening to Haggai. Here is the gist of Haggai's message: wake up and get your priorities straight. "Give careful thought to your ways" (Hg 1:5). With prophetic anointing, he chides them for their preoccupation with their own lives and misplaced priorities. "Is it a time for you ... to be living in your paneled houses, while this house remains a ruin?" (1:4) Amazingly, "the whole remnant of the people obeyed the voice of the Lord ... and the message of the prophet Haggai, because the Lord their God had sent him. And the people feared the Lord" (1:12). They heard, not the voice of a man, but the voice of the Lord. They followed their leaders and put their hands to the task of honoring God's priorities. The Master Builder empowered everyone, from the top down. Progress moved quickly along. The Lord kept up the encouragement along the way.

Looking to Ezra. Let's jump ahead about fifty-five years, to Ezra's call to return to Jerusalem. The first six chapters describe the joyous completion of the work of rebuilding the temple. I find it significant that after the foundation was complete, the altar was given first attention. Upon its completion, sacrifices were offered. Always, our highest priority is to ensure that our hearts are clean before God.

Ezra modeled a quick and unquestioning response to divine initiative: "the gracious hand of his God was on him" (7:9). This man had authentic humility. He was patient to "wait his turn" before returning to the city and people he loved. He watched for the Lord's purposes to unfold, then followed them. Starting the journey with an assortment of adults, children, and all kinds of earthly "stuff," he refused offers from the king for protection. Instead, the Lord honored his faith and protected his endeavors.

There is something instructive here for us today. It is tempting for a reform-minded person to get impatient and jump out in his own strength. *True spiritual reform requires men and women discerning enough to see the need for change, but dependent enough on God to wait and watch for him to execute it.*

Ezra trusted God's timing, and seems to have moved only when touched by his hand. He knew that God alone had the blueprint and the schedule for construction. Friends, in our kingdom-building endeavors, may our fingerprints not be found on the living stones of the house of the Lord.

Here's another encouraging part of the blueprint. We read in chapter 7 that Artaxerxes appointed Ezra to oversee the gathering of further provisions for the temple. Before departing Babylon, the exiles celebrated the Passover a full seven days "because the Lord had filled them with joy by changing the attitude of the king of Assyria, so that he assisted them in the work on the house of God" (6:22). Think about this. When God is at work, we sometimes see a remarkable synergy of heaven and earth. A God-ordained favor may open doors to the hearts of secular authorities, who come alongside with political support and resources.

Buoyed by the extra support, it was nevertheless Ezra's job to call the people to brokenness before the Lord. As a priest-intercessor, he was willing to stand in the moral gap between the holiness of God and the repetitive sinfulness of his people, and initiate repentance over their persistent compromises. You may be a pastor, church leader, or an intercessor. As you're watching the Lord's house being raised in your area, simply be open to any opportunities to call local saints to repentance. Pray for the gift that Ezra was given, the discernment to put a finger on the problem, and the conviction to call people to honestly deal with attitudes or actions that grieve God in any way.

Ezra models for us a servant in season, carefully watching for signs of God's grace initiatives, and unafraid to both follow hard after God and say the hard thing to men.

Building with Nehemiah. Ezra and Nehemiah were contemporaries. Ezra was the priest-intercessor. Nehemiah was called to fulfill a specific task: to rebuild the broken walls and burned gates surrounding the temple. God inspired Artaxerxes to appoint Nehemiah: "Because the gracious hand of my God was upon me, the king granted my requests" (Neh 2:8).

Approaching his project, Nehemiah inherited a pile of rubble and a host of rabble-rousers. The local ruffians Sanballat and Tobiah ridiculed and scorned the laborers. As work got underway, even the people declared, "there is so much rubble that we cannot rebuild the wall" (4:10). Sometimes, we look at our circumstances, perhaps in a church situation or in assessing the condition of the Body of Christ in our city, and we feel overwhelmed. "Lord, what am I to do with all this rubble?" It can feel like standing at the foot of the Oklahoma City bombing site with only a shovel and a wheelbarrow. We need to assess the reality of the rubble, keeping our eyes fixed on the Source of our strength.

A Call to the Wall

As we distill some of the principles of restoration, may the Spirit bring discernment and insight about the rubble *you* face and show you how to rebuild the broken wall around your own city. There are no physical walls around our cities today. But, as kingdom ambassadors, I suggest we carry a sacred responsibility to maintain a spiritual wall around the places we're called to inhabit. So, what really *is* the wall for us? I believe it is the protection God provides when we walk in covenantal love with him and with others, and walk in Scriptural truth. If we fail to maintain it, through the effects of sin or the neglect of our sloth, our enemy has a legal right to bring oppression into our cities.

If we honor him with our obedience, he covers us, wrapping us about with a perimeter of his presence. In the context of the New Testament church, Paul is assured that "the Lord is faithful, and he will strengthen and protect you from the evil one" (2 Thes 3:3). A comforting promise! But verses 4 and 5 are clear that his divine protection is connected to and conditioned upon our obedience and perseverance.

For you and me, in the here and now, repairing the wall involves dealing honestly with issues of strife and disunity in our congregations, roots of unforgiveness and bitterness in relationships, rampant adultery and divorce in our own ranks, and sexual promiscuity among our young people. It is about admitting that in reality we are not seeking first God's face, but rather seeking first to see the next hot movie or to build up our retirement account or to plan our next vacation or buy the latest techno-toy. How can we presume on God to shield us when our spiritual house is in such disarray? We have some serious repenting to do.

Honest Assessment. Neither naysayers nor idealists are well suited to serve as reformers. We need someone like Nehemiah, who can remove the rose-colored glasses, assess reality for what it is, then approach the problem with optimism and hope. As Nehemiah encountered resistance, looked at the rubble, and processed the complaints of the workers, he took the problems straight to the Lord in earnest prayer.

In some cities the rubble of apathy, disunity, and unbelief is overwhelming. Tensions loom between large-church and small-church pastors, disagreements flare over styles of worship, and "turfism" is rampant. Often there is a longstanding root of bitterness in one of the leading churches tracing back to the departure of a pastor or a church split.

Someone needs to honestly assess the damage. Before any medical doctor can offer an effective remedy, he must have an accurate diagnosis. We need those who can see the holes in our city walls and tell us about them. Often, intercessors, who are posted on the walls of a city, will see the holes. Prayer warriors may sense a burden of disunity, bitterness, or apathy, but may not be able to clearly identify the source of the problem. City-wide consultations of both the gatekeepers (pastors) and the watchmen (intercessors) can help accurately assess the condition of the wall around that particular city.

But such assessment should not be limited to the church and its faults. We must also research and discern specific areas of brokenness in the culture around us, for example racial tension, the breakdown of the family, violence in schools, and so forth. Then we can begin praying together about how to more effectively minister God's healing grace.

Facing Resistance. Besides the rubble, we face other forms of resistance. Nehemiah heard the voices from without saying, "Don't you even dare think about building this wall." And voices from within the camp moaned, "there is so much rubble ... we cannot rebuild the wall." Voices, words, innuendo, negativism—all are intended to intimidate and de-motivate. "What are these feeble pastors doing? Are all these inter-church prayer meetings really worth all the time and effort?"

What can we learn here? First, the role of the leader is to quiet anxieties and bolster confidence in the Lord: "Don't be afraid of them. Remember the Lord, who is great and awesome, and fight ..." (Neh 4:14). Further, Nehemiah wisely placed the workers according to their strengths. He picked out those skilled in hand-to-hand combat, men with physical prowess, and made them soldiers. As leaders, we must put on the perimeter men and women endowed with discernment, courage, and authority to "stand watch" over the construction site. And we have to be ready to move swiftly to shore up a place of weakness, or to resist an assault from both human flesh and the devil.

Prayer Itself Is the Strategy

The most important piece of God's blueprint for rebuilding abandoned altars and broken walls is desperate prayer. When we honestly come to the end of ourselves and earnestly call to him, he then faithfully reveals our next steps. Nehemiah cultivated such a life of prayer that he was ready to hear and receive the Lord's burden to rebuild the wall.

Actually, we can say that prayer itself seems to have been Nehemiah's chief strategy. When frustrated, fearful, or facing opposition, he turned instantly to the Lord. When the gruesome twosome of Sanballat and Tobiah scorned the project and spit in Nehemiah's face, the Lord's construction foreman immediately rang up the Boss (4:4). He didn't get caught in the snares of back-and-forth insults. He did not spit back at the mockers. He asked the Lord to supernaturally turn their scorning back onto their own heads. Recognizing that the opposition is not really directed at him, but against the Lord's authority, he gave his opponents over to God's judgment. As a result of his leadership, the people plunged back into the work with earnest. The gruesome twosome come back at them, this time with "the Arabs, the Ammonites and the men of Ashdod" (4:7), angry and plotting a riot to shut it all down: "we prayed to our God and posted a guard day and night to meet this threat" (4:9). Opposition was turned into an opportunity to demonstrate the sovereign power of God.

Finding supernatural strength. When people begin to move in the will of the Lord, extra strength is released. Again "...the people worked with all their heart" (4:6b). When saints are inspired by a godly leader to put their hearts and hands to work, God's power is "all over them." One of the marks of authentic awakening is the joy and strength of Jesus' presence filling and flowing through his people.

Half of the men continued to work on the wall, and half equipped with "spears, shields, bows and armor" (4:16) were posted as watchmen. Those who transported materials worked with one hand, carrying a weapon in the other. They were ready for both work and warfare. This is powerful. Labors in the natural and supernatural were integrated. Work and prayer were woven together, not compartmentalized.

The wall was lengthy and the workers spread out, vulnerable to attack. Sometimes in the fray of the day-to-day battles, it is just comforting to know that friends of like heart and call are posted on the wall, watching with you over the landscape of the Body of Christ rising from the rubble. Nehemiah instructed them that when they heard the trumpet, they were to rally together at a particular place on the wall. When we gather in a city for prayer and worship, we may issue specific calls to pray about such areas of vulnerability.

Nehemiah led confidently, proclaiming "Our God will fight for us." He stationed key people at the lowest and most exposed places. Sometimes we need to rally to pray for a church in trouble, or give cover to a key leader under assault. We may need to rise up and pray over divisive issues and disputes in our local government, or intercede in the aftermath of a community trauma, such as a school shooting, natural disaster, or a murder. Recall the power of united intercession in the aftermath of the catastrophe of Oklahoma City.

City leader, pastor, intercessor, influencer, have you seriously assessed the condition of the spiritual wall around your city? Is there a church facing a split? Is there a congregation in dispute with city officials over a building permit or approval to start a Christian school? Have local saints been lulled to sleep by the intoxicants of worldly culture? *Might someone need to blow a trumpet and shake people out of their apathy, calling them to the weak places on the wall?*

Recently, in an area where I serve as a consultant, three local pastors came together to proceed in the spirit of Matthew 18 to go to a colleague to talk about issues of spiritual abuse in his life. A core group of intercessors, briefed on the situation, supported the effort in prayer and supplication. This had been a weak point of the spiritual perimeter of their region. The confrontation was difficult, and at first not very well received, and yet the Lord brought an answer to the prayers. The issues finally came out into public view, and the brother resigned his pastorate, having to honestly assess how he and his church had broken trust with members of Jesus' Body.

When we get serious about rebuilding the wall of protection around our cities and counties, we can expect the adversary to put up a fight. Because our walls are made of love, obedience, and righteous living, our downfall often comes in the form of strife and unrighteousness. Let's be diligent to put these principles into practice, and follow the wisdom and ways of Nehemiah.

Returning to Righteousness

Any awakening that is authentic will be evidenced by a practical concern for relieving the sufferings of the poor. Right in the midst of the wall-building project, Nehemiah exposed a significant pocket of local sin, and railed at the Jewish hierarchy for it (see Neh 5). Finding themselves in famine, people had been forced to mortgage their land to secure food, to borrow funds to pay the king's tax, even to sell their children into slavery to their countrymen. Nehemiah confronted the sins of usury and slavery, and demanded that it stop. People emptied their own pockets to relieve the burden of the underprivileged. To free up additional resources for the people, Nehemiah himself refused to receive the allotment of food and provisions normally provided a governor.

With all the talk about "revival ... awakening ... visitation," whatever favorite buzzword we like, we run the risk of over-hyping an expectation that to really be moving in God, we need to be experiencing major, miraculous supernatural activity. If that's our goal, we may fail to minister God's mercy to the real needs of people in the here and now.

Recently I spoke at a pastors' lunch in Salem, Oregon, sharing my heart for building unity and praying for breakthrough. At the close, a pastor approached me, a man who has invested most of his life in this city. "You know," he shared haltingly, "I agree with what you're saying, and would welcome anything the Lord wants to give us, but on the road to breakthrough, what does the Lord require of us? Doesn't he give us his heart in Isaiah 58, where he describes the authentic fasting and praying he is looking for?"

If you do away with the yoke of oppression, with the pointing finger and malicious talk, and if you spend yourselves in behalf of the hungry and satisfy the needs of the oppressed, then your light will rise in the darkness, and your night will become like the noonday.

ISAIAH 58:9b, 10

The brother had a point. The heart of God beats through this entire chapter: clean up your own sin, take care of the poor, administer justice in your city, and I'll turn your darkness into light, I will call you "Repairer of Broken Walls, Restorer of Streets with Dwellings" (12b). Building a city-wide prayer movement is not only about celebrations, church growth, and great conferences, but more about being fully available to our Lord to heal the brokenhearted, feed the hungry, and set captives free. Let's carefully guard against a view of reform that is romanticized and over-spiritualized. In most cases, it comes down to the plain hard work of incarnating Jesus' love—giving a drink of water in his name without a thought of getting anything in return.

We may invest a lifetime praying for our church, city, or nation. We may find ourselves blessed to be a Simeon, who finally saw the child of promise in his advanced age. Or we may live out a life of discipleship, suffering, and dying without ever having touched any great move of the Spirit. Our call is to be faithful, and to leave the ultimate results of our obedience with God.

Repenting of Corporate Sins

At the completion of the wall, the Israelites enjoyed an unprecedented weeklong celebration of the Feast of Tabernacles. The people came before the Lord to openly confess their own sins, and the sins of their fathers. Nehemiah 9 shows us clearly that both the leaders and the people exposed significant and long-standing "stronghold issues." They got down to the real roots. For a quarter of the day they read the word, letting the truth expose sin and disobedience. For a quarter of a day they confessed their sin, and worshiped. Then the Levites, standing on the steps, called out to the people, "Stand up and praise the Lord your God" (9:5).

Renouncing Social Injustices

The authenticity of what happened in the spirit was immediately evident in the natural. The people were ready to make right their moral wrongs and compromises. They had already renounced the practices of usury and economic servitude. Now they committed to forbid their daughters to intermarry with men of the local, foreign culture (10:30). They committed themselves to not buy or sell on the Sabbath, and to financially support the ministry of the temple. The bottom line was an oath of holy obedience, "We will not neglect the house of our God" (10:39).

What Are We Looking For?

If we're in any measure serious about opening doors for spiritual awakening, we have to be ready to separate ourselves from the corruptions of our culture, and be a witness that the values of the kingdom really can work in a fallen world. Can we not learn from such a powerful, old covenant model as this one, and walk in the spirit and substance of it in our day? We've just looked at a real life, old covenant illustration of corporate restoration. With the covering of the blood of Jesus, his personal intercession on our behalf, and the power of his indwelling Spirit, we have more than enough to radiate his life into the dark corners of our desperate cities.

So, what can we learn and apply here? God's favor and blessing are released when we get to the real core of our spiritual compromises, confess them, and resolve to walk in the truth. Honest, desperate prayer is efficacious in drawing forth divine power. I believe our Lord is graciously giving us opportunities to put these things into immediate practice.

The more I read and meditate on Nehemiah, the more I get blessed by the tangible results of authentic spiritual reformation. I've said that Ezra and Nehemiah's chief strategy was desperate prayer. Check out a few of the dramatic, very measurable results that followed their obedience. Should these breakthroughs surprise us?

- At the dedication of the wall, the Levites were "sought out from where they lived" to come and lead worship. People *went looking for the worship leaders* to bring them into the presence of the Lord! (12:27)
- The joy of their celebration was so exuberant, they could be "heard far away" (12:43). *Appreciation and praise erupted* in response to the goodness of God. Their joy was uninhibited, loud, inescapably noticeable.

- The people were "pleased with the ministering priests and Levites" (12:44b). The people of Judah were *verbally and visibly supportive of their leaders,* and showed it in their actions.
- All Israel "contributed the daily portions" to support the temple workers (12:47). *People opened their purses* to give first fruits and extra offerings to the work of the kingdom.

The exiles returning from bondage in Babylon were broken and humbled. They were hungry for the familiarity of home. In his graciousness, the Lord provided a vision for a return. He raised up gifted leaders—secular politicians, apostolic builders, prophets, priests, worship leaders, and a host of willing people—and called Israel back, not so much to a place, but to himself, the only true source of peace and spiritual prosperity.

When we see people in our congregations supporting leadership, showing up for worship and prayer gatherings, making their time and energy available to serve, and joyously offering finances, you know beyond any doubt that the glory of God is breaking in. And when leaders and lay folks in healthy congregations catch sight of the biblical blueprint for building a city-wide church, we can begin touching together new places of divine grace. In an increasing number of locales, I believe we are today poised to hear God's call and to prepare places for his habitation in this 21st century of church history. As this drama unfolds, it will indeed be "his story."

Chapter 4

Giving Leadership to the City-Wide Church

I've been speaking in general terms about our Lord's intent to dwell more fully in our lives. I'd like now to explore more concretely what a living, breathing city-wide movement of prayer looks like. How does one church, expressed through diverse congregations, really work?

While principles and patterns exist, the resurrection life of Son and Spirit emerge through a variety of contextual adaptations. Our Lord does not "move" a standardized product, like vitamins or kitchenware. He's not producing prayer movements with a cookie cutter. Let's stand in awe of the spontaneous and often surprising creativity of the Master Craftsman!

What Are We Expecting?

In November 2000, Mission Houston sponsored a "think tank" for city-reaching leaders from cities of varying sizes around the United States. Everything from seeking the manifest presence of God to the realities of needing money to make all this work was avidly discussed. *If* the hand of God is on it, and not our human fingerprints, a city in spiritual breakthrough that is moving toward transformation will see:

- spontaneous increase of prayer that is united, fervent, and sacrificial.
- a heart unity of its spiritual leaders.
- functional cooperation between these leaders and the governmental, educational, and economic gatekeepers of the city.
- a team of pastors and para-church leaders who are guiding a comprehensive, biblical vision to incarnate the presence of Jesus to every heart, home, and socio-economic sphere.

City transformation involves a "critical mass" of saints filled with the life of Jesus who are impacting lives at every level of the local culture. As a result of their intercessory prayer and increased righteous living, the region can expect a measurable reversal of crime. Such social ills as domestic violence, teen pregnancies, alcoholism, and drug activity decrease dramatically. The curse of racial superiority is broken as Hispanics and Asians, Blacks and Jews, Caucasians and Native Americans worship and walk together as "one new man" (Eph 2:15). Congregations see themselves as the "church of the city," serving on the same team, with the same goal. Their pastors have favor with the mayor, city council, police chief, business leaders, and the university president, and have freedom to bring the influence of the gospel to bear on the culture. A widespread knowledge of the person and presence of God touches a high percentage of the city's populace.

Is this a classic case of "pie-in-the-sky, bye-and-bye" here? I don't think so. The first Transformations video documents Almalonga, Guatemala, as a stunning case study of a city that once was dark but now is light, a place once bound by alcoholism and occultism, which now has a Christian population of over 85 percent. The secular press in Guatemala now refers to Almalonga as "the city of God."

I believe that God is uniquely preparing such cities of refuge, places of his presence where he can model concrete answers to the impassioned plea of his Son recorded in John seventeen.

Leadership Is the Key

To reach our cities, the Lord is like a CEO looking to select and empower choice management teams. God delegates to us the responsibility of serving as his "vice regents," endowed with authority to advance his kingdom. Gifted men and women, whose shared vision inspires others to follow, are rising into leadership roles in numerous city contexts.

John and Charles Wesley, with their band of "Methodists" in eighteenth century England, model for us the kind of spiritual leadership I am talking about. They were available to God for a reformation of spiritual life that resulted in conversions, radical holiness, and social change. Historians agree that the Methodist Revolution helped to spare England from a devastating equivalent of the French Revolution. The Wesley brothers provided a minimal organizational structure to maximize the move of God, forming "classes" and "bands" to sustain what God had initiated. Without necessarily duplicating the same structures today, we would be wise to discern and implement organizational models that are effective for giving both depth and breadth to a reformational work of the Holy Spirit.

Leadership at Every Step of the Way

Having been privileged to be involved in this sort of work now for more than a decade, I would describe the objective of a city-wide prayer movement as follows:

> *To promote a fervent pursuit of God that attracts his favor and results in loving unity and a revival of the Body of Christ across denominational, ethnic, and cultural lines, such that out of the unity and frequent worshipful prayer will emerge God-breathed strategies that minister his grace and mercy to the city.*

From my experience, I have identified some of the steps in the birth and development of a city prayer movement:

1. **Pray concertedly for God to birth a movement of prayer in your city or area.** Typically he stirs pioneer leaders and intercessors in a local setting to call the Body to return to Christ as first love, repent of sinful compromises, and hunger for spiritual awakening.

2. **Hear and heed what the Holy Spirit is saying to the Church.** Listen carefully for what is on God's heart for his Church. Sort out authentic revelation from all the latest good ideas. Tune into what the Lord is saying and doing in local prayer meetings or in other city and regional prayer movements.

3. **Challenge the "city elders" to united, concerted prayer**. Typically, a catalytic individual or core of leaders will call their colleagues to begin seeking the Lord through united prayer and worship.

4. **Increase the unity of the leaders in your city.** Set aside extended periods to seek the Lord (Ps 27:4, 8), and to "live together" (Ps 133:1). Cultivate a covenantal commitment to model the unity of Christ's Body (Eph 4:1-6; Jn 17:21-23). Secure a perimeter of godliness through repentance and accountability. And begin seeking together vision and strategy for more effectively reaching the community.

5. **Identify and empower servant leaders to guide the emerging movement**. These individuals, typically a mix of pastors and para-church leaders, are responsible to define, deepen, and broaden the movement. They are to model mutual submission, honoring one another in humility. They seek consensus for advancing the vision for a city-wide movement of prayer. Eventually, these leaders will define a comprehensive, on-going strategy to reach the city that is measurable, sustainable, and collaborative, i.e., "the whole Church taking the whole gospel to the whole city," until Jesus returns.

6. **Identify, affirm and assign local intercessors** to "watch" over the city in prayer (Is 62:6, 7). The emerging "city elders" call mature prayer warriors to the wall of the

city to offer the Lord repentance for the corporate sins of the churches and the culture; to pray for the strength and protection of pastors and churches; to seek God for the release of revelation of his purposes for the city; and to petition God to expose and weaken strongholds of darkness rooted in the city.

7. **Research the historical and spiritual background of your city.** Ask the Lord to raise up individuals motivated and gifted to dig out data and to develop understanding of the spiritual and cultural foundations of your city or region. The purpose for gaining this information is to better inform and focus intercession for the city (see appendix 7).

8. **Plan appropriate "catalytic kingdom events" for the Body.** Once a movement of prayer is birthed, leadership is responsible to discern ways to deepen and broaden the movement in the hearts and minds of the "people in the pews." Such events may include city-wide prayer and praise gatherings (see appendix 5), pulpit exchanges, worship celebrations, solemn assemblies, observance of the National Day of Prayer, prayer training seminars, etc.

Real examples. While there are principles and patterns that guide this process, there will always be contextual variety in how the principles are applied. One example: in 1995 in Marin County, California, a major stronghold of both materialism and New Age spirituality, a core of leaders emerged with a deep passion for prayer and unity. For two years they collaborated with adjacent Sonoma County for an annual Prayer Summit, until the movements in both counties were strong enough to stand on their own.

In 1997, "Mission Marin" was formed, with a vision to unite churches in this spiritually hostile environment to more intentionally walk together in the John 17 witness of oneness. They formed a Pastors Servant Leader Team (PSLT), and began to seek God's mind for the county. Later, a core group of mature intercessors, recommended by the pastors, formed an Intercessory Servant Leader Team (ISLT). They have encountered endless challenges, bumps in the road, turmoil in the churches, and spiritual counterattack. But here's the key ingredient in this model: a core of both pastors and prayer leaders committed to stay the course, a clearly designated PSLT leader or "point man," and a core group of five women that give leadership to the ISLT (see appendices 2, 3 and 4).

Another example: Melbourne, Australia is a culturally diverse metroplex, comprised of thirty-one municipalities. Several key intercessors were actively praying for the city long before a "gatekeeping team" was formed. In 1996, International Renewal Ministries helped launch a Prayer Summit for Melbourne, with encouraging initial results. However, a servant leader team was not clearly appointed to guide the movement. The interest of greater Melbourne pastors waned and momentum slowed. By May, 1999, it was clear that it was essential for the local leaders to re-ignite the vision and passion for a Prayer Summit and to select a leadership team. This occurred at the close of an August, 1999 Prayer Summit. While each separate municipality is responsible to raise its own city team leadership and cast its own vision, a greater

Melbourne team is now beginning to give broad visionary guidance to efforts to move forward in prayer, worship, and outreach.

Spiritual Leadership Roles

Ephesians 4 lists the five callings of leadership given to the church to grow us up into the fullness of the life of Jesus: apostles, prophets, evangelists, pastors, and teachers. We have understood well the job descriptions of evangelists, pastors and teachers. Men and women in abundance serve the Body in these roles. What has been far less understood are the roles of apostle and prophet. There is still a great measure of dis- agreement and controversy over these roles. As it relates to birthing and building city-wide prayer movements, let me share a few thoughts.

Prophetic Ministry
A prophet tunes his ear to hear the word of the Lord. This often comes through a specific Scripture, a vision, or a com- pelling impression from the Spirit. It might be a correction, an encouragement, or a warning, or it may provide under- standing of what the Lord is doing. While creative in tone, nuance, and imagery, a prophetic word will never contradict the written word or compromise our Lord's character. Such "words," whether spoken in a public or private setting, must be tested by pastors, leaders, and other prophets.

When the roles of apostle, prophet, and priest work together, as portrayed in Haggai 1 and 2, spiritual anointing is released in fullest measure. The apostolic leader is in a position of authority and responsibility, but he has an ear open to God's voice speaking through the prophet. The priests serve as motivators and implementers, stirring the people to follow a vision.

I believe we're beginning to see the timely restoration of the apostolic and prophetic roles. I'm confident, in spite of the theological suspicions and tensions concerning these offices, that they are being restored to put the Church in right order, restore it to health, and maximize the gifts and callings of the Holy Spirit to bring in a widespread harvest. I pray that the Father will clarify his appointing and anointing of the apostles and prophets among us, refine their character through trial and testing, and position them in the Body for this current season of kingdom expansion.

Understanding the Apostolic Role

Whether we use the term "apostle" to refer to an office, a spiritual function, or both, I believe we can determine some characteristics of those who wear this "mantle." Apostolic leaders are spiritual pioneers, always pressing on the outer edges of kingdom expansion. The very meaning of the word apostle, "sent one," indicates that an apostle is one who moves into a new situation, culture, or nation with an authority to proclaim the gospel, advance God's kingdom, and help set the church in right order.

The Lord is painstaking in his refinement of those whom he chooses as apostles. An apostle, therefore, is one who has often been severely tested, broken, and humbled.

Further, apostles often have a special degree of faith to believe God for miracles and to "go for it" in the face of resistance. The apostolic leader, bold but not reckless, sees out ahead and has courage to "take the point." As a safeguard, the apostolic leader is accountable to the collective consensus of a team of leaders.

In the context of the city prayer movement, apostolic leadership is typically provided in one of three ways: (1) a local pastor carries the city-wide mantle in addition to leading a congregation, (2) a small group of apostolically anointed leaders submit to one another in the form of a council, with one among them taking the functional role of setting meetings and casting vision, and (3) someone comes in from the outside to give occasional input, to consult, to teach, and to help troubleshoot obstacles. Much of what I do is to visit cities to encourage and mentor local leaders. The Spirit often gives me insight to see things and authority to say things that help bring definition, order, and fresh momentum. But the proverbial "buck" stops with the local leaders who are responsible to sustain the health and growth of the city-wide church.

It is imperative that anyone with a prophetic or apostolic gifting is respectful of and responsive to the perspectives of local church leaders. And yet, while honoring such leadership gifts, we must guard against a top-down elitism, and build checks and balances into the process of getting God's mind for his Body in a regional context.

Forming City Leadership Teams

I am deeply indebted to DAWN Ministries (Discipling A Whole Nation) for their excellent work in defining a strategic process that guides the leaders of a city to walk effectively together. Jack Dennison, in *City Reaching: On the Road to Community Transformation*, traces the development of the DAWN strategy from its origins in the Philippines with founder Jim Montgomery, to its current application to city-wide prayer movements. This strategy, in my opinion, lays down the best biblical "tracks" to both sustain and measure the ultimate success of a city-reaching endeavor. Too many movements put the proverbial "cart" of events and tactics before the "horse" of an ongoing strategic vision. This typically results in a large consumption of time, energy, and resources, with disappointing results and a consequent vacuum of vision. Strategic vision inspires and sustains over time, and produces measurable fruit.

At a consultation for city-reachers in Houston in February, 1999, George Otis shared a word picture. "Once a spark of faith has lit the fuse of potential city transformation, the challenge is to keep the fuse burning to a point of ignition." To keep the fuse burning, a regional move of God needs leadership.

We must embrace a vision that centers on the primary aspects of the kingdom: uniting in prayer, worship, mercy, and evangelism. A movement can all too easily slide out of balance and become overly charismatic—or too cautiously conservative. Wise leaders will keep vision fixed on the central mandates of the gospel, and maneuver the flow of the movement past extremes. Individual pastors are free to be who they are and flow in their own traditions. But when we come under the "big tent" of the body of Christ, our liberty must be tempered by sensitivity.

A visual picture will help here. This spectrum has served as an "aha!" experience for many emerging city- and area-wide movements:

COMMUNITY TRANSFORMATION:
Keeping the Fuse of Faith Burning

Old Mindset	New Mindset	City Leaders Emerge	Acceleration	Visitation	Transformation
• Isolationism	• Living in unity John 17	• City church identify, "one church, many congregations"	• Signs of "seismic spiritual activity"	• Sovereign favor of God empowers our endeavors	• Measurable change of a city or region

0 — 3 — 5 — 7 — 10

Scenario	Signpost	Initiatives	Indicators		
• Status quo	• Pastors praying	• Research begins	• Presence of God		
• Desperate cry of a pastor intercessor, or faithful remnant	• City-wide gatherings	• City-wide prayer mobilization	• Prayer that is united, sacrificial and fervent		
	• Pulpit exchanges	• Vision defined	• Spontaneous conversion growth		
	• Reconciliation (racial, intra-church, denominational)	• Connection with key influencers	• Signs and wonders		

God's Presence and Power

A Faith Fuse Is Lit

While this spectrum may appear simplistic, it is helpful in assessing where a city is or isn't in the process of spiritual transformation. Let's be honest: *apart from divine intervention, it is a very long road from 0 to 10.* Currently, #3 range prayer beachheads abound. Many places are seeing signs of life and stirrings toward John 17 unity, devotion to prayer, and reconciliation. This is a good thing, but without leadership, this activity can disappear quickly from the radar scope, and fade to a mere sentimental memory of days gone by.

Many places are still stuck at 0, entrenched in an old paradigm mentality: "I do my church thing, you do yours, we catch a monthly ministerial luncheon together, and respect one another from a distance." So many pastors long to see something new, but are disheartened by the lack of interest. *So what can you do to get out of the old paradigm doldrums?* Several things.

Take initiative to pull the embers of kindred hearts together to cry out to the Lord to bring change. We may be talking about only three to five people here ... Go for it! Plant good seed in the soft soil of pastors and associates who are open to breaking out of the status quo. For example, provide books, videos, newsletters, and tapes that touch on what the Spirit is saying to today's church. Ask someone already in the prayer movement to come to your town for a vision-casting session with local leaders, and toss in a free lunch. I have been invited into places where it looks like only a small pile of straw has been assembled, but I only need to touch the tinder with a torch!

Unless the Lord Builds the House

Identify the geography you're responsible for, consolidate your core remnant, keep calling your colleagues up to a compelling biblical vision, and offer the Lord your desperate prayers. Then wait, watch, and play "follow the leader." Let the Spirit of God unfold what to do next. If it isn't clear, wait some more. Don't try to *make* anything happen out of season.

Many cities today are moving into stage 3 activity. A new spirit of camaraderie and common mission fills the air. But as they try to make "next steps," in the absence of leadership, these cities hit a wall, fall back, and languish. I've seen cities stay in a fallback mode for years. This kind of building requires an initiative of apostolic-style leadership that hears God, sees the vision, and blows a trumpet. Most often, one of two scenarios develops: (1) a pastor or para-church leader with the most passion for these things rises and calls his colleagues to step up to the vision, or (2) a small core of leaders of like mind and kindred spirit begin to pray and dream together. But if someone with apostolic gifting—a leader among leaders—does not clearly emerge, someone typically begins to lead by virtue of either a spiritual gifting of leadership or a natural talent for organization. If this is all that you have, that's okay. Go with who is going.

There's something important here. Building the Lord's house, living stone by living stone, must be done in God's order. He is looking for the "elders in the gates," the spiritual shepherds of the city, to stand in a place of authority. These elders, with a mandate burning in their own hearts, can then move in the following kinds of directions: one by one, meeting by meeting, letter by letter; putting the watchmen in place on the walls of the city (in most cities, the intercessors are longing for this, and looking for the pastors to act); drawing in key influencers—gifted laymen, businessmen, political and community leaders; calling the body of Christ together for united prayer and worship.

There is a common difficulty. Most leaders are reticent to assert themselves over their peers, thinking, "who am I to take city leadership?" It may come off as self-promotion, pride, or posturing. Sometimes this deferential "walking on eggshells" around one another goes on for years, and bogs a movement down. Sometimes a leader knows this internally, and has already heard from the Lord. Other times, peers may be the source of affirmation and encouragement. Sometimes there's a solo leader who hears the Holy Spirit and starts to blow a trumpet. What is most common is to find a small core of two or three pastors who carry the seeds of this vision, who pray and say together, "What if other pastors caught this vision and joined us? What could happen here?" This is often a form of emergent leadership that is interim in nature. Such a core typically becomes its own ad hoc envisioning team, refusing to let the vision fall to the ground. *Any city that hopes to move from a hopeful beachhead toward spiritual breakthrough must have persevering leaders who keep the fuse burning.*

Pushing Forward

There is a critical point in this journey. A city may fail to formally acknowledge this new level of leadership, and fall back—back to events that have worked in the past, back to prayer meetings that lack focus and fire, back to a Prayer Summit or leaders' retreat with diminishing participation.

Momentum is lost, and hearts begin to sink.

To maintain momentum, there must be a formal acknowledgement and appointing of these leaders. Ideally, this should happen in a setting where there is an established foundation of united prayer and worship. A solid quorum, a representative cross section of city leaders, must be present to "choose ... men ... who are known to be full of the Spirit and wisdom" (Acts 6:3).

Selecting a Leadership Team

An ideal quorum of city leadership is present at either a Prayer Summit, leaders' retreat, or special half day of prayer. The leaders taking the time to pray become the catalytic core that selects those who will intentionally steward a city church vision.

Over ten years, I've led a simple selection process that has proven to work quite well. First, I explain clearly the role of a city servant leader (see appendix 3), and what the commitment really involves. There are other names for this role, e.g., "city church facilitators," the "not-so-highly-exalted-kahunas," etc. In one city this group is called, surprisingly, the "steering committee" (I thought that's what my father chaired at church in 1958!). Anyway, the name is not as important as a clear understanding of the role, and the integrity of the selection process.

When the role is clear, I'll call for a time of prayer and reflection, followed by this instruction: "Look around the room, and write the names of five to seven individuals you discern have a passion for prayer and unity, and a mantle to steward what God is doing in our midst." This process, and the affirmation of one's colleagues, can put a leadership team in place.

Some groups use an open nomination process, but this has its hazards. It may become a personality contest. Someone may be suggested who really doesn't qualify. It may be tempting for some to say "yes" and difficult for others to say "no." The privacy of a ballot, after prayer and reflection, seems to me to secure the best result.

These leaders can then move forward to steward ongoing prayer and worship in the city, and seek the Lord for his unfolding of vision and strategies. Within six to nine months, it is wise for this team to hold an overnight retreat to develop an initial "VisionPath" for the city movement (see a VisionPath model in appendix 8).

Selection of city leadership can occur in other ways. There is no patent on the above process. The regional Church of the Valley movement in Oregon is comprised of two counties, with over eighty participating churches located in six towns of differing size and culture. In January 1998, our leadership team determined that we could no longer effectively "drive" a city reaching vision for this whole area, so we decentralized. As the point man in Corvallis, I began to pray about who should serve on an emerging team of leaders for "the CitiChurch of Corvallis." Through letters and announcements at prayer meetings, we set a date when our local pastors would choose this team. Seven leaders were selected and served as an "interim envisioning team" until the Prayer Summit in February 1999, when these seven were confirmed and two others added.

Another example: Eugene and Springfield, Oregon are two "sister cities" to the West and East of Interstate 5, surrounded by the smaller towns of Lane County. At the time of this writing, their emerging leader team crafted this phrase, "United in

Purpose, Distinctive in Vision." The churches of the culturally diverse cities in Lane County can unite on the broader purposes of a regional movement of prayer (a regional "big tent"), but have freedom as individual cities to raise up their own local leaders and define their own vision (city-wide movement).

Facing the Hard Issues

There are some major adjustments as we move in these new directions. It all can look great on paper, but we're dealing with the unpredictability of human personalities who are interpreting and processing a new paradigm. Here are six key issues that arise quite often.

Affirming and holding servant leaders accountable. Other leaders may have a struggle in submitting to the authority of such a servant leader "council." Church denominational structures might also be suspicious. This is natural. Non-participating pastors or churches might well say, "Who are *you* to discern vision for *my* church and priorities for our ministries?" This is a good question.

However, this kind of new city-wide leadership is not a new kind of governmental authority, but rather a movement of seeking the Lord's heart for ways to cooperate together in kingdom ministries. Servant leaders are aware that they are part of a move of the Holy Spirit to restore unity and vitality to the body of Christ in accord with Jesus' priestly prayer. And because they see themselves as directly accountable to Jesus as Head of his Body, which includes all the churches, they also see themselves as accountable to their peers in those churches as they present vision or strategies. Their primary focus is healthy "body parts," individual congregations flowing and growing in the Spirit, and corporately submitting to the Head (see appendix 3).

Facing the question of women in leadership. Can women be considered to serve as city-wide leaders? Even if it is determined theologically that they *can*, is it advisable in every environment? The debate on the role of women in governmental leadership continues unabated. It has both theological and cultural aspects.

Many excellent books, with sound exegesis, open the door for women to serve as pastors and leaders. On the other hand, for one example, the Southern Baptist Convention closed the theological door on women pastors in the summer of 2000. Some denominations (mainline, evangelical, charismatic, Pentecostal) freely ordain women pastors. In African-American and Hispanic cultures, I often meet husband and wife co-pastors, or women moving freely as pastor-teachers.

Because of the diversity of hermeneutic interpretation of biblical texts as well as cultural differences, we're just going to have to continue to live with this tension, irrigate it with a ton of love and prayer, and patiently work it out in each context.

Well-meaning, sincere Christians will remain on both sides of this fence, with many of us hanging or leaning on the fence in some way. In many cities the mere idea of a woman in governmental leadership stirs debate and division. In these places, it's just not wise to press the issue. The bottom line: let the context and the consensus of corporate theological conscience guide. Seek God's mind, decide, and walk it out in love.

In settings where women are allowed and affirmed to serve, some male leaders still may have theological reservations, or still may be very much in process with their position, but because of their commitment to a city-wide movement, they may choose to extend a loving grace towards women in leadership. We all have "litmus tests," measures of true orthodoxy, personal preferences and opinions. But in choosing to honor one another and to walk together in the wider Body, we can go two ways: we can stretch to be forbearing on an issue of secondary doctrinal importance, or defer to those who are unable to accept women in governmental leadership, and avoid division over the issue. Clearly, the Spirit is superintending and blessing both options as city-wide movements continue to develop. Ultimately, only the Lord himself can arbitrate the interpretive obscurities and complexities of this issue.

Achieving racial, cultural, and theological diversity. This also is an ongoing challenge that requires constant vigilance and forbearance. It is easy enough to believe, think, and say that "we are one in Christ." But when we begin to walk in functional unity, the stress lines show up. In urban, multiethnic settings, it is advisable to begin building authentic relationships in the early stages. Leaders of different class and color must mutually own and steward a vision for a bona fide city church. This all sounds well and good, but many key leaders may not be convinced that this "new thing" is really of God. You can do the best you can do to honor the diversity of the Body, and draw leaders in that represent all the various streams. But—and let's please get this—it is unwise to cave in to an obligatory "tokenism."

We just need to do our best to be inclusive from the beginning, but without compromising the core requirements of the role of a servant leader. Ultimately, we all really *do* need one another! At a recent meeting of city-reaching leaders, one participant shared something quite profound: "As we walk more together, we will wear off one another's eccentricities, and fill up one another's deficiencies." This process is work, but the product is well worth the labor.

Moving the mindset from local to city church. This is another major hurdle. In some environments, the change of thinking can come to a large number of leaders within a matter of months. In other cities, it may take years for other local pastors to see and value the vision, and "sign on." I referenced earlier the "Apologetic for the City Church" produced by the Spokane, Washington movement. This is an excellent tool for bringing the focus back to scriptural revelation.

Let me say again that *the city-wide church does not supplant or replace the local church.* The city-wide church expresses the biblical reality that there is one Body that finds expression in a wide diversity of congregations. Many cities have found it helpful to construct a simple statement of commitment to walk together in covenantal love (see appendix 2). In my own city, we came to the point of asking, "What *must* we do together that we cannot do on our own?" These clear biblical mandates alone provide a compelling case for busy pastors to justify the expense of time and energy outside of their local congregations.

It is also helpful to provide books and videos that unfold what God is doing in cities today. George Otis' documentary *Transformations* videos have, in my view, been the most powerful recent tools in changing the minds of skeptical pastors.

Jack Dennison's book, *City Reaching: On the Road to Community Transformation*, is effective. Francis Frangipane's *The House of the Lord* provides a helpful biblical context. David Bryant's *Messengers of Hope* stirs fresh fervency and fire.

Personnel and funding. In the early stages, there is often a high degree of excitement and energy flowing into the new endeavor. After the initial dust settles, however, there comes a reality check when servant leaders reach the limitations of their own time and energy. Men and women called to the pastorate are consumed day and night with the primary care of their flocks. Para-church leaders also have limits on their time.

In the early building years in our area, one other pastor and I gave considerable time to help establish the Church of the Valley. After several years, we could not sustain it. Having incorporated as a 501 C-3 nonprofit corporation, we asked our pastors to challenge their boards to help fund a half-time administrative assistant, and, in one afternoon, we received commitments sufficient to cover the position. Increasing numbers of cities are looking for funding earlier in the process, and are raising money for at least one fulltime person who can carry the administrative tasks.

It is far easier to raise funding if you construct and communicate a clear VisionPath, defining Mission, Vision, Values, and Goals.[1] It is often appropriate to seek initial venture capital from the business community and to encourage participating churches to include the city-wide movement as a line item in their budgets.

Commonsense leadership. Our Citichurch of Corvallis servant leader team has defined its responsibilities according to personal passion and gifting: regular pastors' prayer; pastoral relations; liaison with the intercessors; LOVE, Inc., (our mercy ministry); school service partnerships; city-wide gatherings; training events. This has helped make the work far more manageable. With these assignments, we're able to maintain effective oversight of the movement.

Here are the basic, bottom-line expectations for a servant leader team: 1) make the monthly meeting, 2) be consistent with regular prayer times for city leaders, 3) show up for and stir your people's participation in city-wide prayer events, and 4) invest time fulfilling specific task group responsibilities, or delegate them to others. Even competent leaders will need to rotate off the team for a year, maybe two, as circumstances dictate.

Here's a snapshot of what the leadership of an emerging city-church might looks like:

LEADERSHIP FOR A CITY-WIDE CHURCH

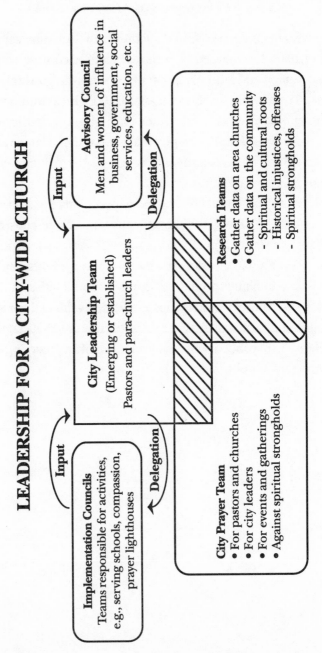

Advisory Council
Men and women of influence in business, government, social services, education, etc.

City Leadership Team
(Emerging or established)
Pastors and para-church leaders

Implementation Councils
Teams responsible for activities, e.g., serving schools, compassion, prayer lighthouses

Input

Delegation

Research Teams
• Gather data on area churches
• Gather data on the community
  - Spiritual and cultural roots
  - Historical injustices, offenses
  - Spiritual strongholds

City Prayer Team
• For pastors and churches
• For city leaders
• For events and gatherings
• Against spiritual strongholds

These basic functions can take a variety of forms and names in different contexts. Appendices 6 and 7 help flesh out some of the practicalities of how pastors, intercessors, and researchers relate and work together. The "Advisory Council" plays a critical role. These individuals may be busy pastors, business professionals, city council members, those involved in the social services, any and all committed to the potential of city transformation. Let the Holy Spirit lead in the definition and formation of these Body-wide roles and responsibilities.

Take note of the shaded areas. There must be intentional, planned interface of these teams to build relationship, to worship, and to dialogue about the unfolding vision for the city. As challenging as this is, it's important to keep these teams on the same "vision page," and at a similar pace. I often recommend that our "CitiChurch" leadership team connect between two and three times a year with the intercessors. Increasingly, seasoned intercessors will pray on site at the annual Prayer Summit. In the evening sessions, they join in for worship, then slide out to their own prayer room. They may also be invited in to share specific Scriptures, words, and prayer leadings they have been receiving.

When teams work together well, we can touch the Father's favor. On the second night of the May, 1999 Summit in Adelaide, Australia, the intercessors joined with the pastors for worship. In prayer, someone referenced the alarming rates of unemployment and suicide among Australian youth. A youth pastor picked up the burden, and a spirit of travail and intercession fell on the whole group. Pastors began to cry out to the Lord, and intercessors began to weep and travail. For about thirty minutes, the Holy Spirit superintended our petitions. At one point a woman pastor uttered a prophetic word that was "spot on" (that's Aussie talk). I recall thinking, "Lord, this is how you want us to be together in your presence, a mixed group, fully available to you, letting you bring heavenly breakthrough."

Let me summarize the context of this chapter with this thought. As we continue to develop innovative models, it is the quality and commitment of leaders that will determine whether a city-wide movement sustains momentum or stagnates. I believe the Lord is watching and waiting to do his part—to release to us the presence and power of his Spirit—if we will rise up and be obedient to do our part.

Chapter 5

The Bottom Line Is Love

Bear with each other and forgive whatever grievances
you may have against one another. Forgive as the Lord
forgave you. And over all these virtues put on love, which
binds them all together in perfect unity.

COLOSSIANS 3:13, 14

Through all the teachings, parables and prayers of Jesus, the
thread of love weaves all other truths into a tapestry. In his
upper room discourse (Jn 14:21, 23), Jesus shared with his disciples that he and his Father would dwell with those who obey
his commands. How do we do this, practically speaking? We
want God to dwell in our hearts and, by extension, in our
cities, but that level of obedience is much easier to talk about
than to live out, isn't it?

Think back for a moment about Nehemiah. Can you imag-
ine, in the midst of the vast project he managed, how much
envy, jealousy, and strife he no doubt confronted, how many
arguments he had to arbitrate for people "bent out of shape"
over one thing or another? Like Nehemiah, most of us live in
the real world, with real feelings and real problems with other
people in our faith community. Because the quality of our
interpersonal relationships matters to God, it should matter

far more to us. Working hard and well at resolving strained relationships is the central qualifier for receiving God's blessing in a city context. We can ramp up all kinds of plans and projects, but if we are not dwelling together in unity (Ps 133), we'll miss the blessing from above.

The heap of unresolved hurts and offenses in the church must grieve God deeply. Doesn't this at least partially explain why many churches and cities do not see Jesus "disclosing" himself in greater measure? The challenge to work at healthy relationships is always relevant to our nuclear families and our church or mission organizations. But I want to apply it to this new paradigm of God's presence in the city environment.

One of my favorite Hebrew words is *chesed,* lovingkindness that lasts a lifetime, a commitment to another that says, "Come what may, I'll stand by you!" When there is disruption in a relationship, God's heart, full of *chesed,* wants you to talk it out, walk it out, reason together, wrestle together, until peace is restored.

Surely when Jesus looks at a city, he doesn't see Baptists, Methodists, Nazarenes, Episcopalians, Presbyterians, or Pentecostals. We're so adept at labeling ourselves—marking out and measuring those things that make us distinct *from* one another. We see one another from the outside in. Jesus, I believe, sees us from the inside out. He sees the presence of his indwelling Spirit that has marked that person as a son or daughter of Abraham. Take down the walls of our sanctuaries, cover the signs that stand in front of our churches, and we see that "we are all members of one body" (Eph 4:25).

Terri and I have lived in Corvallis, Oregon, for twenty-four years, and have given leadership to both the Church of the

Valley (a regional movement of prayer in Oregon's mid-Willamette Valley), and the CitiChurch of Corvallis. We have made it our aim to work hard at maintaining right relationships. This isn't easy. As loving as they may be, leaders will always offend someone by their decisions, style of leadership, or personalities. Leaders become lightning rods for the discharge of people's unresolved pains and problems. Leaders, likewise, can slip out of the Spirit and into their own human reactions.

In the development of our movement, I appointed "Jim" to give leadership to our intercessors. He differed from me in both gifting and personality. We both knew working together would be a challenge. We labored alongside one another for about a year, then the wheels came off. We just didn't work well together. With good intentions, we tried to understand and reconcile our differences.

Eventually, we followed our separate tracks, "moving on," as we say. But our separation did not go unnoticed. Some of his friends wondered what had happened, and why things didn't work. Typically, scenarios like this leave a residue of divided loyalties, "camps" of disillusioned folks who carry around either their own or someone else's offenses.

Somewhere about a year later I ran into Jim and his wife (I'll call her Julie) at a wedding reception. Things were clearly not okay. It felt like two opposing poles of a magnet were moving about the room. We arranged to meet, but we both came away unresolved. I had my perspective. He had his. We prayed together and parted cordially, having done the best we could do. I thought things were as okay as they were going to be. Another year went by. One day Terri was shopping at the local market and ran into Julie. Things were still not okay. There were still others around who didn't understand why we had separated in the first place, and why we couldn't get along now.

I fasted, sought the Lord, and asked him to search the dark corners of my own heart, to expose my own blind spots. I invited them over for an evening. We eased into the issues, revisiting the problems and explaining our perspectives. I sincerely asked them to forgive me for hurting them and sinning against them. Julie bristled. "I can choose to forgive, but I just can't trust you, Tom."

"I understand, but will you let me pray and ask the Lord to change your heart toward me?" She was open to this. As I began to pray, the Spirit touched Julie in a remarkable way. Melting, weeping, she came across the room to embrace both Terri and me. The four of us ended up in a heap, on our knees, soaking in the love of Jesus, reconciled. Praise God, this was not merely a political "détente" (a cessation of hostilities) but a deeper bonding of our hearts.

The emotional resolution and spiritual peace this brought was wonderful. Other close friends, associates, and local leaders were delighted to hear the report. What the devil had designed for evil, the Lord took and transformed for a greater good.

How many Jims and Julies do you have in your sphere of ministry or in your town? What does your own relational wreckage look like? How much might your unresolved relationships hinder the fullness of God's favor from coming to your church or community?

It's important to qualify what I'm saying. It doesn't always work. There *is* no perfect Christian utopian community. In many cases, the Lord deals with people's hearts over time, convicting, softening, preparing them to resolve issues. And sometimes, matters *are* left unresolved, and people do move on. As members of the body of Christ, we must make the admonition of Romans 12:18 our ceaseless aim: "If it is possible, as far as it depends on you, live at peace with everyone." As much emotional work as it entails, we must be committed to extend the longsuffering forbearance of "chesed" to one another over the long haul.

Like the Early Church

As followers of Jesus, we all have longings to be a part of a church, a ministry team, or a movement that reflects the biblical ideal. We often say, "We just want to be like the early Church." While the early Church was awesomely empowered by God and expanded miraculously, it was still comprised of ordinary people, common "clay pots" like you and me, flawed yet still filled with the life of Christ. Just read Paul's epistles and note all the problems. He labored hard at challenging people to walk together in covenantal love.

Paul gives us the model of community life in the book of Ephesians. There are two awe-inspiring descriptions of the Body working together, Ephesians 4:1-16, and 5:15 through chapter 6. In between these portions he writes about what it really takes to get there.

Ephesians 5:18-21 provides an ideal picture of how any body of Christians can function together, portraying the two ingredients that make for a healthy community: (1) submitting to God for the daily filling and controlling of the Holy Spirit, and (2) submitting to one another out of reverence for Christ.

The Spirit of God is the oil that lubricates the joints of the Body. If I allow my flesh (criticism, jealousy, envy, resentment, pride) to show up in a gathering of the body of Christ, I am like grit that grinds the gears of a machine. Likewise, I need to yield my right to be in control or to manipulate others. Our Lord gives grace to the humble, but opposes the proud.

When we are submitted to God's Spirit and to one another, it is no strain to flow together in spiritual community. When these two kinds of submission are in sync, power is released for husbands and wives to live in covenant together (5:22-33), for children to submit to parents (6:1-4), and slaves (today's "employees"?) to submit to and serve their masters (6:5-9). We have liberty in the Spirit to sing, pray, prophesy, worship, and share who we really are, with hearts that spill over with thanksgiving and praise to the Father.

When the Body is rightly ordered, full of the Spirit and the favor of the Father, it can be "strong in the Lord and in his mighty power" (Eph 6:10), taking up defensive armor and offensive weapons to stand against the ways and wiles of the evil one. Then the Lord imparts his authority to his people to proclaim truth that sets captives free, to advance against the strongholds of the enemy, and to further extend the reign of the kingdom. This is true for individual congregations but it is multiplied manifold when it is extended to the city-wide Church.

Together, we can be filled with the Spirit, moving in humble submission, respecting God's order, and progressively displacing the devil. Francis Frangipane describes this succinctly: "It is possible for Christ's church to be so properly aligned with heaven that the Holy Spirit actually displaces the powers of darkness over our cities."[1]

But how do we get to this place of authority and victory, moving from being the Church mediocre to the Church victorious? By committing ourselves to love each other. The strength of a church is rooted in the health and maturity of its relationships.

"Do not give the devil a foothold." Let's focus on two phrases that stand out in Ephesians: "do not give the devil a foothold," and "do not grieve the Holy Spirit." We are responsible to close a door on the devil's attempts to gain footholds in our relationships. The entry point Paul exposes here is anger that remains unresolved. It could just as well be resentment, jealousy, bitterness, or judgment of a fellow believer. If we give our enemy a crack, and refuse to repent of it, his demons work it into a chasm.

Of course we're all going to experience anger. People's attitudes and actions will frustrate and irritate us. If anger, judgment, criticism, or bitterness boil up within me, but I don't let it spill out, I can deal with it in my own closet with confession and repentance. We all know this is not as easy as it sounds.

If my reactions to a brother or sister spill out through a comment or an action, or "boil over" in angry, wounding words, I am responsible to go a step further. I may be right in my opinion, even have the mind of God on an issue, but then sin against someone in how I communicate my position.

Once, in the flow of a local prayer meeting, a talkative pastor wanted to share something. But it was time to move on. I was right to say so, but was just too blunt and abrupt in doing it. Months later, I noticed Roger wasn't showing up for prayer. The Holy Spirit convicted me of my abruptness. I called Roger, repented, asked for his forgiveness for wounding him, and readily received it.

Friends, as small or insignificant as these things may seem, if we ignore them, the devil gets a foothold, making a chasm out of a crack. Bad feelings fester and often pollute others, poisoning their feelings toward the one with whom we are at odds. As members of one Body, with one Head, we are duty-bound to close cracks of animosity in our homes, church fellowships, or in our city environment.

"Do not grieve the Holy Spirit." We wonder, don't we, why we taste so little of the favor and blessing of the Lord in our corporate life? It may be because we're leaving doors open to the devil on one side, and closing doors to the Spirit of God on the other.

Paul is dealing specifically with what comes out of our mouths, telling us that our words should be spoken to bless and build others up. James backs him up, exposing the hypocrisy of praising God and cursing men with the same tongue (Jas 3:10). Paul tells us: "Get rid of all bitterness, rage and anger ... every form of malice" (Eph 4:31).

Every form of malice? Ouch. Any thought or feeling that wishes ill-will toward a brother or sister has to be crucified. You and I have the responsibility to either hang on to our malicious judgments, or hang them on the cross. I am called to forgive others in the same manner as Jesus has forgiven me: freely and repetitively, as an act of my will, letting my feelings follow after my decision to forgive.

We can only practice these things by fully absorbing Jesus' character. If we are faithful in closing doors to the devil, and opening doors for the Spirit's blessing, we can then ask and believe the Father to extend his favor to our community.

Let's apply this to a city context. The Spirit of God grieves when people leave a congregation hurt, angry, and bitter. In any city, there are always a certain number of sheep leaving congregations, looking for better pasture elsewhere. People leave wounded, unresolved, carrying some measure of bitterness, and they carry their "disease" to their new church, which receives them unsuspectingly. But in cities where pastors have chosen to walk together in trust, where they meet regularly for prayer, people find it harder to carry their unresolved attitudes and problems into another fellowship. More pastors are doing "exit interviews," probing for problems, encouraging people to go back and clear up issues. The city-wide prayer movement provides a working context in which there is increased accountability for both shepherds and sheep to walk in obedience to Jesus' commands. (See appendix 2.)

Finding Peace in Our Relationships

When dealing with others who are emotionally healthy and mature, you can speak truth in a loving way, get response, and achieve a sense of closure that both sides understand. But the problem is there just aren't many emotionally whole people in our culture these days. Some people are scarred by life's experiences and lack the capacity to act and react in normal, healthy ways. Raised in homes ravaged by abuse, alcohol, and divorce, they have cracks in their foundations: rejection, abuse, conditional acceptance, wounding words. These patterns make resolution of conflictive relationships difficult at best, sometimes nearly impossible. But with the Lord's healing love, and time, and a lot of prayer, miracles do happen.

Paul tells us, "If it is possible, as far as it depends on you, live at peace with everyone" (Rom 12:18). There are two helpful implications here: (1) it is not always possible to find peace with everyone, and (2) I can do my best to resolve my issues, but I cannot force someone else to do the same. I must be willing to believe that anything is possible if God is in it, and to give reconciliation my best effort.

We have to accept the fact that some people are so damaged by life experiences that their wounded souls lack the capacity to resolve conflict in a healthy manner. Damaged people carry with them emotional "tripwires" that set these self-protective patterns in motion. The less healthy person wrestles to understand why no one seems to understand him or her, and the more healthy person suffers from the tension of wanting to resolve the conflict.

Sometimes, the best that can be done is to make sure your own heart is right. Through fasting and earnest prayer, I need to let the Spirit "dredge" up things in my self-life that are incompatible with Jesus' character. I need to ask others: Is my demeanor too harsh? Am I unapproachable? Share with me any "blind spots" you see in my life. Often we just need to give the other person the benefit of some space, time, and prayer, in the hope they will come to a deeper level of self-understanding. If they cannot or will not "get it," then we must leave them where they are, and go on.

Let's also understand basic differences in personality. We can choose to love and appreciate people we do not necessarily "like" naturally. We won't mesh with everyone. There will always be "irregular" people who grate on us. God is honored when "irregulars" choose to function together in a team environment. But it is okay for conflictive personalities to keep their distance, practicing forbearance in love.

Let's also acknowledge our differences in gifting and calling. Pastors, for example, have an altogether different internal makeup from intercessors or prophets. We must free ourselves from the expectation that we can and should all feel and act the same. Let me suggest a few practical steps we can take towards closing a door on the devil, and opening a door for the irrigating streams of healing love.

Follow Jesus' Instructions

It goes without saying that we need to follow the Master's model. If you are at the altar and remember that a brother has something against you, take initiative, go to him and seek reconciliation (see Mt 5:23-24). If someone sins against you in word or deed, Jesus tells us to first go directly to the person, show him his fault, and try to work it through (Mt 18). If that first effort falls through, you are then free to take one or two witnesses with you to document the offense. If that doesn't get a response (and presumably the witnesses agree with your action), a person's unrepentence can be brought to the whole assembly. In too many situations, we talk to someone else *about* the offending party, rather than going directly *to* him or her. Jesus also told us that if you are praying and you find something in your own heart against someone, you are obligated to forgive (Mk 11:25). This is unilateral forgiveness, regardless of whether the offending party is asking for it or not. If we hold on to judgment and bitterness, not only our prayers will be blocked, but also the Father's willingness to forgive our own sins.

God is so interested in our welfare that even if we don't keep short accounts, he sometimes moves in a sovereign way to help us. In November 1997, during one of our quarterly Church of the Valley Concerts of Praise and Prayer, I issued a challenge: "if you know of any wrong attitude in your heart that would hinder the Holy Spirit from pouring himself out in our city, then come forward to confess and deal with it ... if you need to speak to anyone here, or make a phone call, or commit to contact someone after you leave, let's get our hearts clear before God." I sat down. Unplanned, a woman stood and sang 2 Chronicles 7:14, without instruments. Instantly, people began to flock toward the front, falling on their knees, huddling in small groups, stretched out on the steps. I was drawn into praying for a woman who had left our church with unresolved relationships. Hundreds of needy, honest saints "prayed through" issues that evening, processing the painful stuff of life's disappointments and misunderstandings, and slamming doors shut on the devil.

Pray for the right opening and timing. Unresolved relational conflict may be so oppressive that you just want to go immediately, meet with the person, and get it over with. We lose sleep over these things. But sometimes your own heart is not yet ready, and you need a season of preparation and softening. Or the other individual may not be ready to receive and hear you. Pray, seek wise counsel, wait, and watch for the clear leading of the Spirit to pick up the phone or jump in the car.

Get real. Paul says to "put off falsehood and speak truthfully" with our neighbor (Eph 4:25). I saw this in action in the early 1970s as I watched my mentor, Paul Dekker, in his counseling ministry. Paul would always draw truth out into the open, no matter how awkward or even embarrassing. He did it diplomatically and discreetly, but in a direct manner. Resolving conflict is like going after cancer in surgery—you need to dig, probe, and cut until you're sure you get it out.

Be slow to speak, quick to listen. Resolve to listen well first before you speak. Ask questions that give people freedom to share what is really on their hearts:

"What, specifically, did I do to offend you?"

"What are you really feeling about me?"

"What can I do to regain your respect and trust?"

If your conversation gets stuck, ask the Father for his help in finding resolution, and then give him an opportunity to work.

Agree to disagree. The tension and estrangement in a relationship may have been centered around a particular issue. It is altogether possible to honor the Lord by making peace in your relationship, even if you are still at odds over the issue. It shows maturity to be able to honorably disagree and still respect someone. Freedom to move on may only come when it is agreed that it is okay to differ. At the same time if you are in a staff or team relationship with this person, it might not be wise to continue working together.

Unilateral forgiveness is okay. Sometimes my heart, ready to forgive, meets a stone wall. If a brother or sister just doesn't see his or her fault, you still have the option of extending the grace of forgiveness anyway. The instruction of Romans 12 is very clear that a wrong response can and should be countered with a right response in the Spirit. We are not to judge. We are not to take revenge. We are to model Jesus' heart by forgiving, even blessing our offenders and abusers (see Rom 12:17-21).

Yearning for New Testament Community

Dr. Larry Crabb has captured an important point in his book, *The Safest Place on Earth*:

> Only when the perfume jar is broken in the presence of accepting community is the fragrance released. Everything in spiritual community is reversed from the world's order. It is our weakness, not our competence, that moves others; our sorrows, not our blessings, that break down the barriers of fear and shame that keep us apart; our admitted failures, not our paraded successes, that bind us together in hope.[2]

Our God is always searching for a place to dwell, a people whose hearts he can inhabit and through whom he can show himself to a broken world (read John 14:23 again). When we learn to love each other and live in God's grace, our dreams of dwelling with others in covenantal community can be realized.

Our obedience, flowing out of humility, attracts the glory of God. It can also attract the enemy's attention. Let's take an honest look next at discerning and dealing with spiritual warfare in cities which enjoy heightened levels of prayer, worship, and unity.

Chapter 6

Maneuvering Through the Minefield

Do not be deceived, Wormwood. Our cause is never more in danger than when a human, no longer desiring, but still intending, to do our Enemy's will, looks round upon a universe from which every trace of Him seems to have vanished, and asks why he has been forsaken, and still obeys.

C.S. Lewis, *Screwtape Letters*

If you are serious and intentional in believing God to transform your city or region, opposition is a given. Enemies rise up to resist the work of the kingdom—always. A good portion of this resistance traces to unresolved tensions in personal relationships. But there are other landmines to watch for. If we're going to be effective over the long haul building a city-wide prayer movement, we need to get better and quicker at discerning and dealing with the wiles of the devil, particularly those that put pressure on the internal strongholds resident within the Church itself.

In September, 2000, prayer mobilizers from many of Oregon's cities gathered near Salem for the second "Open Heavens Over Oregon" consultation. We heard some inspiring reports of dramatic changes in the spiritual atmosphere of several Oregon cities.

Ten years ago, Grants Pass was a southern Oregon city filled with logging and recreation industries, wealthy retirees and assorted New Age groups. It was regarded as a "pastor-killing community," and its churches were weak and divided. Through a series of Prayer Summits in the mid-1990s, the emergence of a group of intercessors, and bold leadership among the pastors, a commitment grew to contend for biblical unity, to establish a kingdom beachhead, and pray toward possessing the land.

Sweet Home, a gateway city for Cascade Mountain recreation, was once known for having one of the highest levels of domestic abuse in America. I did a lot of ministry there in the early 1980s, and I discovered the entrenched darkness: Satanism in the schools, sexual abuse, and rampant drug use. Most churches struggled, in isolation, to make any kind of dent in the darkness. In the mid-1990s, the "watchmen on the walls" of Sweet Home and a group of other intercessors from Victoria, British Colombia, began to cry out. They sought the Lord to break the strongholds of apathy, religion, and unbelief. They prayed, "Lord, change our pastors, or move them on!"

Well, the turnover was astonishing. New leaders began moving in. A handful of pastors started to pray together regularly. Pastors and intercessors began prayerwalking the city, repenting for its sin, and reclaiming ground. A church that had been boarded up was reopened as an interdenominational shelter for homeless and abused women and children.

In the late 1990s, a core of pastors started praying together weekly. Now the police chief, fire chief, city manager, and newspaper editor are professing Christians. At this writing, people from about a dozen churches gather every Sunday night to seek the Lord for revival. The lights are being turned on in a place once known for its pervasive darkness. Today, when I drive through Sweet Home en route to the mountains, I can literally feel the difference in the spiritual atmosphere.

But when spiritual progress like this is made, the powers of darkness are provoked. Anywhere the kingdom of God begins to advance, the devil presses back. Our adversary, motivated by jealousy and vengeance, is the chief robber baron. We are called to carefully and wisely maneuver through the minefield of spiritual resistance that comes when saints begin to expose long-standing strongholds of darkness.

Welcome to the realm of warfare paradox! In the early stages of spiritual breakthrough, mud-slinging should be an encouraging sign for those who can see with eyes of faith. The prophetic handwriting on the wall irks the powers of darkness.

No Weapon Will Prevail

Before we look at some of the landmines that Satan plants in city-wide prayer movements, let's anchor ourselves in the bedrock of a vitally important truth: the sovereign authority of God over evil. Satan is a created being, powerful and cunning to be sure, a creature who does insidious things—but he's on a long leash of divine control. Consider this enlightening word penned by Isaiah:

"See, it is I who created the blacksmith who fans the coals into flame and forges a weapon fit for its work. And it is

119

I who have created the destroyer to work havoc; no weapon forged against you will prevail, and you will refute every tongue that accuses you. This is the heritage of the servants of the Lord, and this is their vindication from me," declares the Lord.

ISAIAH 54:16, 17

This is essential truth for leaders, prayer warriors, evangelists, missionaries, and spiritual pioneers. Satan, demonic princes, or wicked men execute destructive plans. While God neither authors evil nor directly controls its hideous outcomes, he does promise to work out a mysteriously redemptive bottom line "for those who love him, who have been called according to his purpose" (Rom 8:28b).

A right understanding and practice of spiritual warfare must be rooted in this perspective. For only by grasping this truth can we believe that "no weapon ... will prevail." Our enemy forges and uses all kinds of weapons: fear, intimidation, dissension, bitterness, sexual temptation, deceit—whatever he deems most effective in any situation. But if we learn to discern the use of these weapons, turn immediately to the authority of the Lord, and put up the shield of faith, flaming arrows are extinguished (see Eph 6:16).

Yes, there are casualties. Men and women often pay a great price for standing at the front of a kingdom advance. Some fall prey to Satan's devices, and are taken out of the battle. Others may be beaten up, pressed down, and crushed by fear and defeat, but they gain ultimate victory by their perseverance (See Paul's litany of oppression, 2 Cor 4:7-12.) Remember in the lives of his saints, our Lord has ultimate control over the assaults of Satan. The devil had to ask God for permission to afflict and test Job (Jb 1:12). Look at Paul's testimony: "...there was given me a thorn in my flesh, a messenger of Satan" (2 Cor 12:7) It was given or allowed—by God—to afflict him, with an explicit, divine purpose of keeping him humble! And consider Peter: "Simon, Simon, Satan has asked to sift you as wheat" (Lk 22:31). Jesus had already interceded for Peter, that his faith would not fail, and that his painful sifting would be ultimately used to ground him further in his faith and to enable him to strengthen his brothers.

The ultimate biblical example of this profound truth is Joseph's statement to his conniving brothers: "You intended to harm me, but God intended it for good" (Gn 50:20). In embracing the trials and testings that come our way, and responding in faith, we allow the Lord to work out his perfect purposes through our own pain.

Returning to Isaiah, we read that the heritage of the Lord's servant is to refute false accusation (Is 54:17). As adopted children, we have to learn to take initiative to speak and act in our Father's authority to expose and refute enemy accusations. This is a matter of maturity, growing in responsibility to discern the ways of the evil one and to deal with them straightway. Paul makes it clear that we release divine power to repel satanic assaults when we raise the shield of faith, speak the word ("rema," a spoken word) as a sword, and call on the Lord in prayer (Eph 6:16-18).

As our Lord graciously brings us new outpourings of his presence, and as the devil brings resistance, kingdom authority must be increasingly released through men and women walking in faith. Certainly the pastors and the elders of local assemblies have authority to deal with the darkness in their own fellowships. But in the context of an emerging city-wide church, I believe God is raising up men and women to discern and deal with the schemes of Satan designed to sidetrack kingdom advancement.

Sweeping the Minefield

What does spiritual warfare resistance look and feel like in a city environment where the Spirit of God is on the move? I want to identify a few landmines I've discovered through experience, and share some suggestions on how to disarm them, (i.e.: what to do before or when one blows up). As we do this, let's be careful to not give the devil credit for all the difficulties that come at us. There are all manner of things bound up in our own impure hearts—unbelief, competition, bitterness, control, malicious gossip, to name but a few—that muddy the waters of the Spirit flowing into the cities and regions we are called to occupy. I'm convinced that most of our warfare traces to ground we yield to the enemy through unconfessed sin (see Jas 3:13–4:10).

In my first book, *The Believer's Guide to Spiritual Warfare*, I offer many examples of personal oppression and how to respond to it. Without duplicating that material here, I want to identify a few specific evidences of spiritual warfare pressure that characteristically arise in an environment where there is increased intentionality of unity, prayer, and evangelism.

Oppression. While the devil is cunning, he is not all that creative. Often, he will stage frontal attacks on one's emotions that are blatantly obvious. In our humanity, we're very prone to fear, anxiety, emotional discouragement, and depression. Evil spirits look for "pressure points" to exploit. Their aim, simply, is to either scare us off the construction site, or debilitate us.

It is not uncommon for pastors, prayer warriors, or their families to come under an unexplainable but altogether real cloud of oppressive heaviness, like a heavy quilt dropped over your head from out of nowhere. Only the anointing of the Holy Spirit's power is sufficient to lift a spirit of mourning and despair, and replace it with spiritual joy (Is 61:3). Strange things flood the mind and emotions. We're often left wondering, "Lord, is this just my own worry and apprehension, or is this a scud missile from hell?"

Fear is common. Fear of the failures of my own flesh. Fear of inadequacy. Fear that if I rise up to pray or be bolder in my witness that I'll get slammed. When hit with fear of any kind, learn to more quickly apply biblical injunctions: to call on the Lord in prayer, to ask him to sort it out, to minister his peace to your mind and heart, and to move by his Spirit to thwart the enemy's activity.

Intimidation. Intimidation—feeling outnumbered and overpowered—leads to spiritual hopelessness ("things will never really change here") and emotional exhaustion. If you are leading the charge in a stronghold region, you can count on intimidation and its various effects. It can manifest as depression, a terminal case of the "quits," or relentless feelings of futility. Learn to more quickly recognize these symptoms in yourself and others, and respond together with faith and prayer.

On the first day of a Prayer Summit for the leaders of Marin County, California, Jesus gave us a significant breakthrough in worship and unity. We had momentum. Marin, just over the Golden Gate from San Francisco and home of the Star Wars studios, is a stronghold of worldly wealth and alternative religions and is one of the more unfriendly climates for evangelical Christianity.

When we regathered for an evening session, the worship suddenly went flat. As we sat going nowhere and getting restless, one pastor went to the kitchen, noisily fumbled in the cupboards, and began making coffee (when in doubt, have a cup). Bill Berry, leader of "Mission Marin," caught my attention, asking with his eyes, "Okay, do you have a clue what's going on right now?" Actually, I *did!* The Holy Spirit had just brought to mind Mark 11:23, where Jesus instructs his disciples to pray to remove mountains. I had an immediate impression that we were rubbing up against a mountainous resistance to God's kingdom in Marin, that something in the demonic realm was angry about this retreat and was manifesting itself right in that room to shut it down. I heard the Spirit of God: "Identify this mountain of resistance, and instruct these gatekeepers to unite in prayer and ask Jesus to weaken and remove it."

I broke into the restless silence. "Brothers, there's a hideous darkness of some sort that doesn't like what we're up to here. It seems like the enemy just sent a torpedo into this room. It's as if something just sucked the life out of the place. Anyone tracking with me?" One after another, the men opened up and began to share what it had been like to try to advance the kingdom in Marin County. Many mentioned being stirred with strong faith when preparing sermons, only to feel weak and powerless in the pulpit. Most admitted to feeling small and insignificant. Others confessed temptations to find another assignment outside of Marin. All agreed that some formidable spiritual presence was sucking life, vision, and faith out of them. Humorously, someone identified this dreaded beast as "the suckage monster," a demonic vacuum cleaner that drained the saints of spiritual vitality. After this enlightening time of sharing, I called the men to come to the center of the room to lock arms and to resolve to stand together against the darkness—and to keep standing. We closed the evening, arm in arm, singing our hearts out, "Victory in Jesus," and "All Hail the Power of Jesus' Name." While these leaders had to go home and face the same giants, the revelation of this stronghold, alongside the commitment to stand against it *together,* sealed a new resolve and strength for building the kingdom in Marin over the long haul. Some three years after this encounter, the corporate resolve to overcome has remained strong. On March 30, 2001, the saints of Marin met together for "One Voice," to praise and pray into God's vision for one church walking together in a place of seemingly overwhelming opposition.

Responding to Oppression

If the enemy doesn't attack you in this way, he'll try to get at a spouse, child, or colleague. The fact that the tactic is common and obvious makes it no less effective. After you get a discerning grip on what's going on, stand and energetically shake off the heaviness, the "wet blanket." Many times, I have prayed, "Jesus, I refuse this irrational, miserable oppression, and in the authority of your name, close the door on the enemy. I ask for your Spirit to guard our minds and hearts, and shield us from all evil. Lord, dispatch your holy warrior angels to come and surround your servants."

The best place to go is Psalm 91, an awesome "if-then" prescription for finding freedom from fear. *If* I dwell, rest, and trust in the Almighty, *then* he will deliver me, he will cover me with his wings, he will make his faithfulness to be a shield about me, and I will not fear the terror of night nor the arrow by day. *If* I make the Most High my dwelling, *then* no harm will befall me, and he will command his angels to guard me and my tent.

If we truly anchor our hearts in his sovereign strength, then only that which he allows can touch us. Choose to believe that. I love the simplicity of the closing promise: "Because he loves me," says the Lord ... "I will protect him, for he acknowledges my name. He will call upon me, and I will answer him" (Ps 91:14, 15). When in trouble, call forth his protection, and receive the ministry of the holy, invisible helpers he assigns to us. He wants us to learn to discern the dangers of warfare, and when to call for help. We're in training. The Lord allows, even ordains, real warfare skirmishes to sharpen our discernment and strengthen our faith.

Often, we're just plain tardy in simply turning to God and asking for help. This may sound stupid, but, frankly, we are. *A part of Satan's arsenal is to stifle and suppress the very impulse to pray!* He works hard to keep our arrows in the quiver and our hands from even drawing the bow. If we would learn to call on the name of the Lord more quickly, we'd see the advances of the enemy scatter more frequently.

Warfare is won or lost on the battlefield of the mind and the timely exercise of our spiritual will. Romans 8:28-39 is effective in dealing with fear. Believe it, stand on it, quote it, live it, breathe it. Nothing—no, *nothing*—will separate me from the love of Christ. I am "more than a conqueror" in Jesus.

In the context of the city church, we need to be looking out for one another, being sensitive to "pray in the Spirit ... for all the saints" (Eph 6:18). As the Lord comes to dwell in our midst and as the devil seeks to attack and counterattack, let's keep a watchful eye on one another, being quick to wrap others about with the shield of faith. In many prayer settings, I often ask the pastors and the intercessory watchmen, "Has anyone been struggling with oppression? Does anyone want prayer to break the enemy's resistance?" This is a simple but necessary discipline to build into our routine.

"Bombs in the backyard." Some mines and mortars go off close to home. We all hate this kind of spiritual warfare, but it happens to all who are called to aggressively advance the kingdom through prayer, worship, missions, or evangelism. Work diligently to get your marriage and family in order. Of course we've all got our flaws; we're a people in process. We'll never be fully free in this life of imperfection and struggle. But to press into city-wide warfare with obvious holes in your primary relationships may lead to unnecessary casualties.

Demonic forces target key leaders, looking for weak areas and pressure points. Unresolved family-of-origin issues that resurface in our adult lives as "character cracks" are vulnerable. Besetting sins of bitterness, sexual addiction, anger, and pride are highly targetable. It is important, therefore, to earnestly seek healing for childhood wounds, scars on the soul that inhibit emotional health. And it is imperative that we be held accountable in repetitive areas of personal struggle.

No doubt many of the marital breakdowns among pastors and leaders trace to warfare pressure. The adversary seeks to drive wedges of mistrust, bitterness, and anger into our relationships. Considering the power that can be released through a husband and wife praying into the same kingdom vision, it is easy to see why the enemy will work overtime to shut down these potential "power cells."

It is normal for couples to have tension over such matters as childrearing, sex, in-laws, and money. Most couples discover differences in these areas and may argue about them on occasion. The pain and drain of dealing with a problem child fits here. Or how about conflict in a job environment that drains your "joy tank"? These things don't enter our "spiritual warfare" column unless they provide the enemy with an opening.

You know it's warfare when a small, normal disagreement suddenly escalates into a serious argument, charged with uncharacteristic anger or venomous words, followed by prolonged periods of distance and avoidance, with both husband and wife losing peace, sleep, and spiritual productivity. A demonic chill can quickly settle in over a marriage. Negative, destructive thoughts take over. Times like this are straight from the pit, and quickly put you "in the pits."

Dismantling the bombs. If there really are major issues you and your spouse need to walk through, then face the issues and work a plan to resolve them. But if the core of your relationship is strong, you may need an increase of discernment and the boldness to exercise authority in closing a door to the enemy's darts. Be aware of your vulnerable areas and be accountable to one another. Make a commitment to talk through conflicts, not letting the sun go down on your anger (Eph 4:26, 27). Resolve to bring your problems to the throne in prayer together. The devil is always roaming about looking for footholds. Take initiative to close the doors to his entry points and to open doors for the grace of God.

Be genuinely willing to bring your life to the Cross, day by day. Marriage is life's most effective crucible for character building. Every time I respond to Terri out of my flesh instead of in the grace and control of the Spirit, an unsanctified part of my life is exposed. Do I justify it? ("I was right!") Do I deny it? ("I was *not* angry!") Do I shift the blame? ("You really are to blame!") Or do I ignore it, avoiding opportunities to resolve the conflict or going silent?

The adversary looks for cracks in my character to exploit. He can only use what I yield to him by my pride and rationalization. James prefaces his instruction on resisting the devil with this reminder, "God gives grace to the humble..." (Jas 4:6). Develop the discipline of resolving conflict quickly—keeping short accounts, talking out your feelings, owning your sin, having a heart that is quick to forgive your mate, thereby restoring the peace of God in your home.

Pray, "Lord, help me learn to discern." As we encounter and work through various conflicts, we will learn discernment. There will be times when you will find relief from oppression through repenting of your sin. Other times, you will need to actively resist and close the door on the enemy. (Chapters 6 and 7 of *The Believer's Guide to Spiritual Warfare* are very helpful in this area).

Let's not forget about the "bombs in your backyard" that are aimed at your children. So many choice servants of the Lord have hearts weighed down by the burden of a prodigal son or daughter. At Prayer Summits, this is *always* an area of need. You may have a child who is overtly rebellious, or uninterested in spiritual things. Keep connected vertically to the Lord, horizontally to your troubled kid, and listen for cues. But where spiritual warfare is concerned, *you can and must take authority on their behalf to plead with God to either shield them from evil, or minimize its damage.*

Your prayer might sound something like this: "Lord, in Jesus' authority, we ask you to keep your hand on Andy. Grant him mercy and grace to wake up and disconnect from his peers and their drug habits. Father, dispatch angels to guard him. Expose and weaken the enemy's schemes in his life. We claim Andy for redemption, in Jesus' name."

Since being called to warfare and city-reaching ministries, I have faithfully and regularly prayed the promises of Psalm 91, 102:28 and 103:17, 18 for my children, Josh and Melissa. Terri and I are responsible to give them the best spiritual covering we can. Leaders carry an inherent responsibility to be diligent and vigilant in praying covering for their spouses and children. But even with this, there is no guarantee against the vulnerabilities of the self-will and unwise choices of others we love.

If you're single, whether never-married, widowed, or divorced, you face a unique set of vulnerabilities. You may struggle with feelings and fears of rejection that may also be pressure points in spiritual warfare. Disappointments in relationships, unresolved hurts, and broken trust need to be healed. You need healthy relationships with friends of both genders. You will also need a special vigilance in bringing your sexual desires under the Spirit's control, a huge struggle in a world saturated with sensuality. Watch for these tripwires, cultivate the disciplines of the inner life, and keep accountable to a friend, pastor, or prayer partner.

Those of us who are married need to take extra initiative to encourage and include singles in the wider family of God. The real key to sealing the cracks that are open to satanic accusation is to be anchored in one's identity in Jesus (Rom 8:28-39; Eph 3:14-19).

Finally, I just want to re-emphasize the importance of Paul's word to "...be alert and always keep on praying for all the saints" (Eph 6:18). Advancing a supernatural kingdom calls us to the highest level of vigilance to watch for danger, and diligence to keep on praying for any and all brothers and sisters vulnerable to spiritual attack. In the analogy of real warfare, no one is ever closer than someone alongside in the trench when under heavy fire. The time has come in our cities to cover each other in prayer.

Laodicean Lethargy

The landmines of spiritual compromise and complacency are, I believe, the most serious spiritual warfare issue we face. If anything can diminish and deaden God's presence in our lives, it is this love affair with the world. Listen to James: "You adulterous people, don't you know that friendship with the world is hatred toward God?" (Jas 4:4). Jesus was disgusted with the self-sufficiency of the Laodicean church (Rv 3:14-22). He counseled them to wake up and put salve on their eyes to see their condition. He rebuked and exhorted them to repent of their prideful self-sufficiency, and open a door to renewed spiritual communion with himself.

Everywhere these days, saints are battling with the tension between the incessant busy-ness of our culture, and the desire to be about the Father's business. There is a constant competition for our attention, and many of these things seem like good, necessary endeavors. But our heart's desire must be to "not conform to the pattern of this world, but be transformed by the renewing of (our minds)" (Rom 12:2).

Worldliness is a spiritual cancer. Two of its symptoms in the Body of Christ are apathy and unbelief. The seductive, polluting powers of pride, greed, and sensuality deaden authentic spirituality. We lose faith that the church really has the power to touch and transform the culture. We hold fast to a belief in the truth of the Bible, but fall prey to a pragmatic agnosticism, unconvinced that the truth we profess really has power sufficient to make a difference.

Through prophetic preaching and desperate praying, may the Spirit bring us to our spiritual senses. If we don't turn our hearts toward the Lord in supreme affection, I feel he will need to turn us over his knee to get our attention.

Dealing with value pollution. Truth decay and the seepage of value pollution is, in my view, our enemy's most insidious scheme to subvert the authentic life of the kingdom. How can we possibly hope to build the house of the Lord on the site of a toxic waste dump?

If we are to have any hope of having heaven invade our mundane lives, we will have to see a critical mass of God's people repent of our compromises with regards to money, sex, and intellectual pride. This will inevitably involve serious lifestyle choices to separate ourselves from the cravings for malls, money, and media, and embrace the values of the kingdom we profess to represent. There is nothing inherently evil about material things. But preoccupation with earthly "stuff" dulls our spiritual senses.

Discerning and Dealing with External Strongholds

I have intentionally focused on internal stronghold issues that plague the Church and rob it of victory and power. But we also have to contend with the reality of external strongholds. In every environment, the influence of particular principalities of darkness leaves a residue of spiritual "air pollution" that affects the local populace, Christians and non-Christians alike. We're poisoned, to some degree, whether we know it or not.

For example, Los Angeles contends with the obvious pollutants of sensuality (Hollywood and the pornography industry) and pride (elevation of human ego through the media). Two influences seem to dominate the Seattle area: humanism (do your own thing, your own way) and New Age metaphysics. Sydney, Australia, though a spectacularly beautiful city, gives special place to homosexuals and hosts an annual Mardi Gras Celebration that opens doors of debauchery. Jerusalem is filled with an intensity of argumentation and violence, as Satan's princes of religious deception vie for control of the "air space" over a place chosen for prophetic destiny. Examples like these could go on and on.

Two observations: First, it becomes important for pastors and intercessors who are gifted with discernment and well informed from local research to get a "read" on the kinds of spiritual influences that operate in their areas, and exercise together a watchful guardianship for the body of Christ. There will be times in prayer gatherings when it is needful to pray for a "breaking and a shaking off" of these external demonic influences from leaders and congregations.

Second, the Lord may initiate an appropriate practice of what I have defined as intercessory prayer warfare—the release of God's authority and power that diminishes the influence of darkness in an entire city. For an in depth development of this level of warfare intercession, see Chapters 6 and 7 of my earlier work, *Breaking Strongholds*.

Pressing On

In the face of spiritual warfare, our predictable response is outright alarm. We need to seriously re-tool our thinking here. If we're pressing a kingdom agenda, let's not be surprised when something ugly presses back. This is real war! James helps us here: "Consider it pure joy, my brothers, whenever you face trials of many kinds, because you know that the testing of your faith develops perserverance" (Jas 1:2, 3). Joy? That's right. It's purely paradoxical. Dirty tricks and testings are a clear sign that the satanic powers are threatened and are throwing all they can back to stop praying saints in their tracks. So let's keep our eyes fixed on the finished work of the cross, and resolve to persevere...come what may. Remember C.S. Lewis's *Screwtape Letters*—head demon Wormwood's greatest angst was the poor frightened believer, floundering and feeling utterly forsaken—choosing to trust God in spite of his circumstances.

Rise and Build

So, wherever you're planted—rural environment, small city, or major metroplex—you have a choice: to stay with the safety and predictability of the status quo or to see where God is going and rise in faith to go there at any cost. The Father, Son, and Spirit are seeking places of corporate habitation in the hearts of those hungry for his manifest presence. The devil is seeking to topple our endeavors like the proverbial house of cards. King Solomon's grand query still rings down through the centuries, "Will God really dwell on earth with men?" (2 Chr 6:18).

Taking steps to intentionally build a city-wide house of prayer is a clear sign that we are serious about our invitation to host a visitation of Royalty. Let's explore next what this might begin to look like.

Chapter 7

Varieties of City-Wide Prayer

"Prayer is the slender nerve that moves the arm of omnipotence."
Jonathan Edwards

I've made about a dozen trips to Australia for Prayer Summits, conferences, and consultations in a number of cities. There are a number of "Aussies" who have become my good "mates" over the years. I've come to appreciate a characteristic of Australian culture—hardnosed pragmatism.

"Down under," if something doesn't work in the real world, as inspiring as ideas and innovations may be, they are suspect. Aussies, along with most Americans, I suspect, want to see the results of prayer investment.

My wife Terri describes prayer as "the irrigation system" that brings the life and power of the Spirit to bear on all that we're about, cultivating the life of the "inner court," that provides power to minister in the "outer court." We must learn how to open the sluice gates of heaven's reservoirs and release a flow of living water into our hearts, homes, congregations, and cities.

Filling the Bowls With Incense

David says something intriguing about prayer in Psalm 141:1, 2: "...may my prayer be set before you like incense." Could it be that David literally "set" his prayers before the Lord? We know that prayer is communication with God and that it builds a relationship. But could it also have substance, weight, spiritual volume? Perhaps it is more than a nice thought or wispy intent.

Cornelius, a godly Gentile, "prayed to God regularly" (Acts 10:2). In preparation for a sovereignly arranged visit from Peter, an angel appeared to him and said, "Your prayers and gifts to the poor have come up as a memorial offering before God." In John's Revelation, we are given a vision of the Lord's throne where the four living creatures and the twenty-four elders are playing harps (perpetual worship) and holding "golden bowls full of incense, which are the prayers of the saints" (Rv 5:8).

So there are "bowls," receptacles of some kind, in the presence of God that collect and store our prayers and petitions? Could it be that these bowls represent certain churches, cities, nations, and people groups? Might there actually be storage places for specific, "designated" prayers? Could it be that when we pray "into" something, our prayers do not just mysteriously enter into God's mind, but are collected and quantified? E.M. Bounds has been one of my chief prayer mentors. Reflect on his thoughts:

Prayer is no fitful, short-lived thing. Prayers are deathless. The lips that uttered them may be closed in death, the heart that felt them may have ceased to beat, but the prayers live before God...

Woe to the generation of sons who find their censers empty of the rich incense of prayer; whose fathers have been too busy or too unbelieving to pray ... Fortunate are they whose fathers and mothers have left them a wealthy patrimony of prayer. The prayers of God's saints are the capital stock in heaven by which Christ carries on His great work upon earth...When God's house on earth is a house of prayer, then God's house in heaven is busy and all potent in its plans and movements.[1]

A tangible, measurable transaction between heaven and earth takes place when I take time—alone, alongside my wife, or with a group of saints—to call on the Lord in faith. If we really believe that prayer is the "capital stock" of heaven, and has the potential for changing things on earth, we'll be motivated to spend more time pouring incense into these bowls. What an awesome privilege! After the bowls are filled with our petitions, the Lord chooses when to make the bowls overflow with blessing (for example: salvation, healing, or visitation).

Our prayers have weight. Let's endeavor to make our cities dwelling places fit for a King, true houses of prayer that continue to refill those bowls in heaven.

Gleanings

Cycles and seasons. In the early days of our Church of the Valley movement, after some of our mountaintop prayer gatherings and city-wide Concerts of Praise and Prayer, many of us assumed that our zeal would spontaneously ignite passion for prayer in our congregations. It didn't quite work that way.

When we begin talking about establishing interdenominational prayer in a city, we need to recognize that most pastors face an uphill struggle, helping their congregations to be faithful in prayer. A pastor may be personally involved in city-wide prayer with other leaders, but he may find the "prayer soil" in his own backyard hard and resistant.

Quite often, increased prayer activity in the city provides a spark that ignites faith and vision in a local church. But each church has its own timetable of readiness for spiritual renewal and its own unique, family system, with its own spiritual history and distinctives, its own potential, its own problems.

Besides, seasons of increased faith and seasons of faltering affect the vitality of a prayer movement. There are times when you sense momentum and hopes are high and times when it seems you've stalled and the irrigation ditches are dry. Learn to identify these human and cultural cycles. Learn to accept them and to work with them until you can press through to the next higher plane.

Case in point: in Oregon, the weather dictates an obvious, annual cycle. We have found that our two best city-wide "windows" for casting prayer vision and planning prayer activities are January through March, and mid-September up to Thanksgiving. In January, people are ready to embrace new

challenges and commit to new causes. We gain our best corporate momentum during this window. Because of our long,
wet winters, once we get nice weather in April, our participation and fervency seems to diminish. I used to be very dis-
couraged by this. Now I just accept it and try to "work" the seasons wisely.

Two kinds of leaders. Over the long haul, if building a city-wide
"house of prayer" is to gain both depth and breadth, two kinds
of leaders are needed. First, each city needs a champion of
prayer, a pioneer, a self-starting motivator who is both passionate about this vision and competent in calling others to it.
This person must have the respect and credibility to call leaders and laity to pray for the city. Secondly, a similar prayer
champion must arise in each local congregation, a man or
woman who trumpets the vision to his or her church, calling
people to participate with the wider Body of Christ. In the
absence of these two key leaders, the growth of city-wide
prayer momentum is hard to sustain.

Spirit-led innovations. A final thought: Prayer leaders should
learn to be innovative in both the structure and style of prayer
gatherings. Avoid old-paradigm prayer ruts like the plague,
for example, drifty prayer meetings with no clear leader or
focus, which tend to get overly focused on prayer for the personal needs of family or acquaintances, or groups where a
strong personality dominates. Leaders, don't do things just for
the sake of change itself, but be creative in following your intu-
itive promptings to try some fresh approaches.

A few ideas: someone can be asked to prepare a particular

focus or to choose a portion of Scripture to pray through. Someone can be designated to lead a time of worship, with an instrument or with just voices, before going to prayer. I have found that beginning with worshipful adoration and affirmation of God's attributes is the best preparation we can make. Someone could read Psalm 130 and call the group to simply wait on the Lord, listening for his instruction and guidance. If a large group gets sluggish, it can be moved into small groups of four to eight with clearly stated prayer assignments and instructions, then drawn back after twenty minutes with a familiar hymn or chorus.

The Spirit of God is infinitely creative, inexhaustible, and fully available to breathe life and power into any prayer meeting at any time, maximizing the spiritual productivity of people's petitions.

City-Wide Prayer Patterns

Let's look at some of the areas of prayer activity in a city context.

Minister's Prayer Fellowships
In many cities, there is a monthly ministerial luncheon where a special speaker brings a word, announcements are shared, and five minutes of prayer are tacked on after dessert. Though I'm all *for* desserts, this is *not* the kind of prayer I'm taking pains to promote. If pastors intentionally connect once or twice a month, *primarily* to share support and actually to pray, a wealth of new options opens up.

The primary objectives of a minister's prayer fellowship should include (1) cultivating deeper relationships, (2) worship, (3) bearing one another's burdens, both personal and professional, and 4) interceding for the churches and the needs of the city. Busy pastors will be convinced to participate if they can connect meaningfully with colleagues in these ways.

The majority of clergy fellowships involve only male pastors. On occasion, I see participation of 10 to 15 percent women pastors or women in ministry. In what we would call the "evangelical" stream of the church (inclusive of charismatics and pentecostals on one side, conservatives on the other, and a lot in between) most pastors are men, with increased participation of women where mainline denominations and multi-ethnic streams are involved.

There are some clear upsides to gender affinity. Men can get more "real" with other men, freer to process their own unique issues. Similarly, women readily identify with each other's particular needs. This is a good and natural thing. In mixed-gender meetings, break-out sessions can give opportunity to process sensitive issues in a same-sex context. But we also increasingly need to be comfortable flowing together in mixed-gender contexts, functioning as a whole, healthy Body.

A Sampling of Models

Jerusalem. In a city known for relentless cultural and spiritual warfare, a group called "Men Meeting with God" has met regularly since 1997 to seek the Lord. At first they met every six weeks for worship and mutual encouragement. Then they began to grow in their desire to pray more frequently for the city and its many unique needs, so they began to meet twice a month. Sometimes, they simply connect with the Lord and one another, followed by an hour interceding for Jerusalem. Other times, they discuss issues distinct to the congregations of the city such as theological tensions, coordinating the many outside conferences that "land" on the city, and disciplinary issues. In September 2000, in the face of another violent Palestinian Intifada and enormous increased stress on Israeli society, a core of leaders committed to two hours of prayer every Thursday morning.

Santa Rosa, California. The pastors of Santa Rosa have logged six strong years of annual Prayer Summits. Between summits, they meet every Wednesday morning, primarily to intercede for Sonoma County. Several women intercessors meet with them for the first thirty minutes of worship, then they move into a separate room to pray. The men rotate leadership of the meeting, having discovered that consistent, responsible leadership is a key to keeping the meetings focused and productive.

Corvallis, Oregon. In February, 1999, the Corvallis pastors determined it was time to intercede weekly for our city. We wrote up a simple covenant that, barring legitimate conflicts, called us to pray together every Thursday morning at eleven o'clock for one hour. We encouraged the pastors to sign if they felt they could commit to this.

On good days we have twenty-five in attendance, on weak days about ten, and on most days, fifteen. A member of our CitiChurch Leadership Team schedules one of the pastors to facilitate each meeting. The leader gives us a clear focus for about ten minutes, and then we move immediately to prayer for forty-five to fifty minutes. We're also working hard at opening this time for women in ministry, pastors' wives, and women intercessors. Recently, we chose to devote prayer on one Thursday each month to the following: (1) a particular church and its leader, (2) a city governmental leader, (3) a school principal or school district administrator, (4) a local business or community leader. On occasional fifth Thursdays, our focus is on Oregon State University, sometimes with a prayerwalk of the campus.

Expect variety. The pastors of each city, county, or region need to decide what works best for their own situation. Experimentation and fine-tuning are healthy signs of progress. The National Pastors Prayer Network (NPPN) is an excellent e-mail resource network in the United States, a forum for exchanging ideas and formats (NPPN.Emailssubscribe@listbot.com). The National Association of Local Church Prayer Leaders offers another networking and learning community opportunity (www.NALCPL.net).

Interceding for a City

Intercession can take a variety of forms, sometimes involving just men, just women, or both. No matter who's doing it, our frequent and fervent prayers keep filling those heavenly "bowls."

Paul shares an exhortation in this regard: "I urge, then, first of all, that requests, prayers, intercession and thanksgiving be made for everyone—for kings and all those in authority, that we may live peaceful and quiet lives in all godliness and holiness" (1 Tm 2:1, 2). The central purpose of intercession is that there would be an atmosphere in a city conducive to the sharing of the gospel, so that people would come to embrace Jesus Christ. Paul goes on, "I want men everywhere to lift up holy hands in prayer, without anger or disputing" (2:8). His point is clear and compelling: don't bicker over doctrine, personality conflicts, or anything divisive. Leaders carry a responsibility to pray about the spiritual climate of their city.

Creative Prayer Formats

Numerous formats continue to spring up at the grassroots level. The Lord gives us such freedom to call on his name in ways that are fresh and new. Here are snapshots of some of the more creative, effective, and enduring formats I'm personally familiar with, ranging from rural countryside to large cities:

Eugene, Oregon. The Community Prayer Network in Eugene is comprised mainly of men and women "prayer liaisons" from a diverse number of congregations. Their pattern is to meet about every two months, each time in a different locale, like a mobile "pillar of prayer fire." The strength of the CPN is the synergistic leadership of three key people: a senior pastor of a small fellowship, an associate pastor of prayer ministries at a large charismatic congregation, and the lead woman intercessor on staff at another large church.

Marin County, California. In another model that works well, five seasoned women intercessors comprise the Intercessory Servant Leader Team, and give direction to about twenty-five women from different Marin County churches. They meet three Saturday mornings each month, spend a significant time in worship, then seek the Lord to discover what's on his heart for the county. Under the leadership of the Pastoral Servant Leader Team, they engage in different intercessory assignments around the county. In the past three county Prayer Summits, a cadre of intercessors has prayed on-site, at points, joining in with the pastors for worship and intercession.

Santa Rosa, California: The city-wide movement in this lovely city has developed a very unique expression they call "CitiReach," a monthly Friday night gathering where pastors and intercessors meet in a different church each month to worship and pray together for the specific needs of the host congregation. When I was there, the pastor offered public repentance for sin in that church that had negatively affected the community. At the close of his sharing, other leaders wrapped around him and his staff, asking the Lord to remove the offense and restore full favor to the fellowship. Praying on-site with each congregation in a relevant way like this is one of the most encouraging tangible outworkings of John 17 unity I've seen.

Toowoomba, Australia: In this "Garden City" ninety minutes West of Brisbane, there is a unique group of believers from many churches who call themselves "Just a Bunch of Christians." They are distinguished by their passion to reach lost people in rather unorthodox ways. For example, some women engage regularly in "mall-walking," discerningly walking shopping malls and looking for openings to talk with needy women about Jesus. One man gave a portion of his pension to fund a coffeehouse for young people. Others organize frequent gatherings for twenty-four hours of nonstop praise, worship, and intercession.

Jerusalem, Israel: In the spring of 2000, a couple moved from Brussels to Jerusalem with a vision to establish a "Tabernacle of David." They started with half-day "worship watches" at different places and times around the city, and are building toward sustaining "24/7" prayer that crosses denominational boundaries. A special worship watch for youth has been added. Mike Bickle, former pastor of Metro Fellowship in Kansas City and now director of the International House of Prayer, is one of the major proponents of this format.

Birmingham, Alabama: In a city with a long legacy of racial strife, Christians have been coming together for united prayer. A racially-mixed group now gathers for what they have called "John 17 Meetings" for monthly prayer in a downtown church. These meetings are part of a "Mission Birmingham" endeavor to unite the whole church to reach the whole city.

Jacksonville, Florida: The servant leaders of "Mission First Coast" launched an initiative on the National Day of Prayer, May 4, 1999. They identified fifty "gates" into the city of Jacksonville: major highways, ports, airports, bus and train stations, radio, television and newspaper headquarters, etc., and assigned pastors and intercessors to pray at each gate and to drive into the ground a two-inch square wooden stake inscribed with Scriptures. Team members took turns driving the stake. No spiritual warfare praying was allowed. Rather, instructions were given to pray blessing on the city, asking for healing of broken families, safety for children, harmony among the races, redemption for the lost, etc. Throughout the day, prayer volunteers drove around the huge perimeter (Jacksonville is the largest geographical city in the United States) seven times in a caravan of cars. Later in the day, all participants met in Hemming Plaza in the city center for united worship and intercession. As a direct result of this day of prayer, violent crime dropped thirty percent in the next eighteen months, the city received an award from the FBI for a reduction of murders, and the number of believers on the city council increased from four to twelve out of nineteen.

New York City, New York: Believers in this large and culturally complex city have pioneered some very encouraging models. Having developed their own annual two-day Prayer Summit model in 1992, they incorporate five one-hour blocks in which ethnic minority leaders share the unique needs of their communities and lead in prayer. New York also has one of the best organized and energetic visions for the annual National Day of Prayer. The leadership team of Concerts of Prayer of Greater New York meet with leaders in twenty locations between January and April in preparation for gathering five to six thousand at the May event. Further, the movement produces *The Lord's Watch,* a monthly prayer guide for over one hundred churches that focuses on four ongoing themes: revival, reconciliation, reformation, and reaching the lost.

PrayerNet Oregon: In the summer of 1999, my wife Terri and I followed the Lord's leading to build a network of prayer mobilizers for our whole state. We put out an initial call, and about seventy pastors and intercessors met near Salem in January, 2000 for a consultation we called "Open Heavens Over Oregon." The following September, we gathered again and formally inaugurated PrayerNet Oregon. In the second gathering, we heard stories from Grants Pass, Sweet Home, Portland, Corvallis, and Prineville. Common to each testimony was the way the Father is working to stir up faith and prayer to change the spiritual atmosphere of our communities. As the Holy Spirit continues to stir and deepen intercessory initiatives like this around Oregon, you can take a look at new developments on the PrayerNet Oregon webpage, www.prayernetoregon.org. (See appendix 9 for other helpful websites.)

United Prayer Gatherings
While successful city-reaching does not center on one-time events, there are times when calling the Body of Christ together under one roof can definitely add spiritual solidarity and momentum to a local prayer movement. Along the way, it can also have its "moments."

Topeka, Kansas. I was invited to lead a prayer conference in Topeka in the winter of 2000. The closing event was a city-wide gathering of corporate worship and prayer for the city. Some leaders were excited and expectant. Others responded with a mix of cordiality and skepticism. Late Sunday afternoon, the pastor of the hosting church shared a concern, "I'm a bit nervous that some of the more exuberant among us are going to dance in the aisles." I assured him that would not be likely.

So much for my prophetic accuracy. By 5:45, the place was jammed, and the multi-church worship team was so anointed that the place exploded with praise. So here I was, sitting up front with the pastor, as young people in the front rows began jumping up and down like happy pogo sticks. Hands were clapping and waving, feet were moving. Within minutes, people were in the aisles, as the saints of Topeka rejoiced in the goodness of the Lord. Sometimes expressions of joy are just plain uncontainable. To be sure, a few leaders were uncomfortable, but almost all were blessed and asked when they could gather again.

Church of the Valley. We held our first official "Concert of Prayer" for the Church of the Valley in January, 1992, led by the innovator of the format, David Bryant. Since that night, our movement has held at least two of these "big tent" gatherings every year. We had been richly blessed for years by David Bryant's original "Concert of Prayer" format, and as time went on we adapted it into what we have called a "Concert of Praise and Prayer." Two formats that have worked particularly well are described in appendix 3; they can be adapted and refined to fit any context.

Practical Details. After a lot of experience with these gatherings, let me share a few practical suggestions. First, it's good to have a facilitation team of three leaders from different congregations who can sit together to "read" how things are going, monitor time and transitions, and make adjustments as needed.

This team should gather all participants together a half hour early to clarify assignments, fine-tune transitions, and commit the evening to the Lord's headship.

Second, it's best to open the gathering with at least thirty minutes of worship. Invite a proven local worship team to provide leadership, adding in instrumentalists and vocalists from other congregations. The main reason for the gathering is to come together to worship God and to intercede together for the city.

Third, I have also found that these meetings need a short, powerful mini-message—not an in-depth teaching, but a relevant, challenging word that stirs inspirational vision and motivation. This should not exceed fifteen minutes. At these events, long-windedness will stifle things quickly—people have not come to listen to long sermons. Our people want to see and hear what God is doing, touch his presence in worship, and pray into his purposes in the community.

Fourth, the prayer segments should be clearly structured. Instruction should be provided regarding focus and time for any preselected participants. Generally, always try to remember the following four approaches: (1) Clearly define a prayer focus. Either tie it to a portion of Scripture or put it on a screen. (2) Appoint a mix of pastors and lay intercessors to step to a microphone to offer short prayers (two to four minutes) for specific areas, for example, unity among the churches, prayers for young people, marriages or families in stress, political issues, prayers for the unsaved. (3) Break the larger group into "prayer huddles" composed of a minimum of six persons each, with clear instruction that prayer participation is voluntary, not obligatory. (Many report that they feel socially "trapped" in these settings. They should be given the option of listening and agreeing with others.) (4) Combine the options. For example, the leader can define a prayer focus, then give an instruction that sounds like this: "We invite you to move into huddles of eight, and begin praying about this focus. Some of you may just want to stay in your seats and pray—that's fine. Others may wish to pray with your spouse or a friend. You may wish to quietly affirm and agree with others' prayers. Also, feel free to come to the front, kneel, and pour your heart out to the Lord." *We need to give people the freedom to find their own level of participation.*

One of the best times we ever had was when we "opened the altar" for anyone struggling with an issue or carrying a burden. First we called forward our pastors and their spouses to serve as prayer teams. When the invitation was given, people came quickly. The atmosphere was charged with faith. For thirty minutes, the worship team "irrigated" this time with gentle worship, drawing in those who had remained in their seats. We had reports later that several had decided at that altar to receive Christ. Marriages were healed, sins forgiven, hearts encouraged.

Leaders should encourage flexibility and spontaneity to allow for the leading of the Holy Spirit on the spot. When God is moving, we need to yield to his initiatives and be open to making "audible calls" at the spiritual line of scrimmage! We must be open to discern where he is leading and willing to go where he is going. In a city-wide group, this takes skilled, Spirit-sensitive leadership. Too much spontaneity, too much exuberance in worship, and your conservatives squirm. Too little, and your charismatics lose interest. These "big tent" gatherings are an innovative art form. We need to keep learning as we continue on the journey.

Tactical Prayer Initiatives

Prayer events, gatherings, conferences, etc. are stepping stones on a city's journey, like points on a map. But to sustain these endeavors over time, we must "connect the dots" with a comprehensive vision that serves to deepen and sustain our commitment to walk together in the spirit of the Great Commandment and to fulfill the Great Commission. With any long journey, there are times when the pace picks up, ground is gained, and hearts are encouraged. But there are also times of fatigue, when achieving the destination looks doubtful. Among the many very helpful prayer initiatives today, here are thumbnail sketches of two of the principal tactical prayer applications employed in many cities.

Lighthouses of prayer. This is a simple, powerful model of prayer evangelism. In the United States, coordinated by the Mission America coalition, it is known as "the Lighthouse Movement." Believers in specific geographical neighborhoods commit to the following: (1) praying for the salvation of unsaved individuals and families, (2) caring for people in practical ways, showing the mercy and love of Christ and (3) sharing the truth of the gospel when trusting relationships begin to open doors.

Prayerwalking. Since the early 1990s, many forms and applications of "mobile prayer" have spread throughout the Body of Christ. Steve Hawthorne, author of *Prayerwalking*, defines prayerwalking as "praying on-site with insight," walking in a particular locale and being sensitive to the promptings of the Holy Spirit. Prayerwalking is a very effective way to get directly in touch with a local environment by using all of your physical senses and spiritual gifts. Prayerwalking enables intercessors to undertake any or all of the following: prayers for the lost, identificational repentance, blessing prayers, intercessory prayer warfare, proclamation of Scripture, etc.

Prayer Events
Finally, there are opportunities to participate in special prayer events throughout the year. (Obviously, my major frame of reference in this book is the prayer movement within the United States. Other nations and regions are developing their own unique initiatives suited to their own cultural distinctives and calendars.)

On the national level, there are two annual events in the United States that provide intercessory focus for the body of Christ. The National Day of Prayer, on the first Thursday in May, has gained significant momentum over the years. The National Prayer Committee sponsors and directs an observance of this event typically televised from four venues around the nation and broadcast via cable and satellite. The city-wide prayer movement in your area can simply provide a facility, tie into the downlink, and participate in a national prayer initiative.

Some years back, Dr. Bill Bright initiated an annual gathering called "Fasting and Prayer," designed to call the body of Christ in America to repentance and sacrificial prayer. Hosted by different cities over the years, such as Los Angeles, St. Louis, and Houston, this gathering is also accessible through cable and satellite hook-ups. Dr. Bright's passionate conviction is that if a critical mass of believers will embrace Solomon's call to repentance (2 Chr 7:14) and enter into sacrificial fasting, the Lord will bring spiritual awakening to America. I have met many men and women who have taken this call seriously.

Permission to Pester

When we look at long-term city-wide work, perseverance is imperative. Jesus' parable of the persistent widow recorded in Luke 18:1-8 commands our attention to persevere in prayer over the long haul. The Master told his disciples "that they should always pray and not give up." This story describes a woman in need of justice trying to get the attention of a judge. He refuses to respond. But because she kept after him, his resistance wore down, and he responded. Jesus makes a very convicting application to the story: if a lonely widow can wear down an earthly, hard-hearted judge, how much more will the saints get response from a righteous Judge whose heart is full of mercy?

We've been given "permission to pester" the Lord with our petitions! Let's appreciate the stark contrast here. The widow was a stranger and she came alone to plead her case. We are the Father's chosen and we can approach him together. The judge kept his distance from the woman, but our Father says "come boldly to my throne." She had no apparent support, yet we have an advocate, the Judge's own Son, who intercedes on our behalf. The widow's persistence provoked the carnal judge to anger. Our persistence in prayer pleases the Lord, and engenders his favor.

Jesus is clearly looking for an intensity of faith and urgency that cries out to the Father day and night (18:7). If we have hopes of moving from a beachhead of prayer activity in our cities toward breakthrough, it will require this kind of persistence. Jesus ends his parable with an unsettling question: "When the Son of Man comes, will he find faith on the earth?"

We can form all the leadership teams we like, set lofty goals, hold conferences, and host reputable leaders—but this cannot transform our cities. Our answer lies not in our endless ingenuity, but in flooding our cities with pervasive and persevering prayer.

Only God can breath on our brokenness and bring forth fruit that ramins. As the Lord searches today for places to dwell, may he be pleased to find hearts desperate enough to persist in pursuing his favor. Will it be greater fullness or falling back? The choice is ours.

Chapter 8

A Touch of Glory

> Surely his salvation is near those who fear him, that his glory may dwell in our land.
>
> PSALM 85:9

In a season of spiritual darkness, we always find a remnant that embraces repentance and cries out to the Lord for a return of his favor. Such cries, heard in recent years across the landscape of nations and cities, sound like the sons of Korah, a desperate plea and a probing question: "Restore us again, O God our Savior, and put away your displeasure toward us ... Will you not revive us again, that your people may rejoice in you?" (Ps 85:4, 6).

What gets our God's attention are humble hearts breaking over sin, yearning for his nearness, and persevering to pray until his glory dwells "in our land." Do we honestly have more than a half-hearted desire for some measure of spiritual refreshment? Or are we so intoxicated by earthly culture that we cannot even discern the departure of divine glory? Are we desperate enough yet to even realize how much we need him? Are we really convinced of the value of unity in a city or regional context? Are we committed enough to believe David's inspired word about the favor of God falling, dripping, pouring out where "brothers live together in unity?" Are we willing to work at being the one church of Christ's Body, comprised of wonderfully diverse living stones of our individual congregations, denominations, and fellowships?

Pillars of the House of the Lord

The foundation for the city-church must rest on the bedrock of scriptural revelation. Our most brilliant ideas and innovations must be informed and ordered by a biblically defined vision that is sustainable over time, or our well-intended efforts will just fade away as just another fad.

Fresh expressions of kingdom community currently underway must be built, in my opinion, on four pillars of enduring truth: (1) historical Christian orthodoxy, including such core doctrines as the triunity of God, the deity and supremacy of Jesus Christ as the sole source of salvation, the authority of the Word of God, salvation by faith alone, and the universality of the Church, Christ's Body; (2) Jesus' "great commandments" to love God supremely and others as ourselves (Mt 22:34-40); (3) Jesus' Great Commission, which sends us into the world to make disciples—teaching, baptizing, and establishing men and women in his truth (Mt 28:19, 20); and (4) our Master's compassion extended freely to those who suffer want or lack (Is 58; Mt 25:31-46; 2 Cor 9).

This universal reality of the "house of the Lord" supercedes all labels and structures we attempt to superimpose on it. When Jesus says "one" in his priestly prayer, he means "one." Although I present in these pages a Protestant perspective of the Church universal, I believe our Lord's Body is inclusive of Catholic, Jewish, and orthodox believers, people of all tribes and tongues who receive his gift of salvation, and are sealed by the Holy Spirit (2 Cor 1:21, 22). Being a member of God's household is thus an organic, not an organizational, reality.

So, instead of laboring only as individual congregations, denominations, para-church ministries and nonprofit organizations, we can walk and work together as one team in a city context to bring glory to God through a witness of our oneness. Individuals, churches, and organizations are equipped with such distinctives as outreach, compassion, discipleship, or counseling for broken marriages and families. But can we not submit such distinctives to Jesus' overarching plea for us to be "one," and to validate his messianic credentials to a needy world?

Divine Openings

If what we're building rests on the four pillars I mentioned, the Lord will be attracted to our yearnings in prayer, and will give us divine openings. One day, while perusing an e-mail bulletin, I read a praise report from Little Rock, Arkansas. The churches had long been stuck in the standard pattern of individual congregations doing their own thing. There was very little unity, and, it was reported, considerable disfavor toward churches from city officials. Having touched God in a profound way in two Prayer Summits, the pastors determined to touch the city with Jesus' love. They called the body of Christ together for a united worship and prayer gathering in November 1998, deciding to pay for all expenses up front, and to receive a sacrificial offering for Little Rock. They also mobilized their people to shore up blood bank levels, and to provide a winter coat for every underprivileged child. They did it. They presented $250,000 to the city government, no strings attached. This marked an astounding turnaround from disunity and disfavor, all in a matter of two to three years.

The inspiration from this idea touched me. I began pondering in my prayers, "Lord, how might you want to impact *our* city with your presence? What is your blueprint for us?" At a planning retreat with the leadership team of the "CitiChurch of Corvallis" in August, 1999, a colleague popped this question, "What would a visible expression of our unity really look like?" We kicked around some ideas. Most were fairly standard and safe. But eventually we began to consider calling our churches together on the highest day of the Christian calendar: Easter morning.

A heightened nervousness settled into our conversation. For a pastor, this is the day of highest attendance and big-time offerings! We went to prayer: "Lord, are you really in this, or is this just another 'good idea?'" To a man, we all felt the Lord was in it. We reached a consensus that this is what he was leading us to do. Please understand, the ability to even ask this question emerged out of years of sincere efforts to live in the spirit of Jesus' great commandments. We were simply beginning to build something on the existing pillar of covenantal love, a steadfast relational commitment that overcomes all barriers and obstacles.

Over the next weeks, in face-to-face settings and through mailings, we shared the vision with our colleagues. We took the idea to prayer in our weekly intercessory gathering for pastors. Consensus spread and grew stronger as others sought the Lord and heard his voice for themselves. By early October, we invited all church leaders to a special night to cast the vision, call people to pray, and challenge them to commit to a John 17 expression of biblical unity. We talked openly about the four "big M's," the message, music, money, and the "munchkins" (all things that hold potential for disagreement and tension). In the days that followed, people in the churches rose to the vision for Easter 2000 with an excitement we had never before seen in our city.

In early December, I noticed an article on biblical unity on the religion page of our local paper, written by Corvallis' local Catholic priest. It so inspired me that I booked a lunch with the Bishop, shared my heart, and laid out the vision for a united gathering of believers on Easter morning to lift up Jesus. He genuinely warmed to the idea, and offered to adjust the time of his Easter morning mass to allow for his parishioners to join in. As it turned out, hundreds of Catholics from the local diocese participated with us. By January, having set our course, our leadership team wrote a letter to the nonparticipating church pastors, warmly giving them opportunity to gather with us. A member of our CitiChurch servant leader team made a personal contact with the key leader of the mainline churches to explain our vision. Having set the doctrinal agenda, we were free to invite others. While none of the leaders of these churches chose to participate formally, some individual believers did.

In April, 2000, the members of twenty-eight out of about thirty-five evangelical churches gathered in the sports coliseum of Oregon State University for EASTER 2000. A full page ad had appeared in the Good Friday *Corvallis Gazette Times,* listing the twenty-eight churches. "WE'RE CLOSING

OUR DOORS FOR EASTER ... and going to Gill Coliseum to celebrate Jesus' resurrection." Our first pillar was in place, agreement on the deity of Christ and the truth of what the Scriptures tell us about him.

Ten days of round-the-clock intrachurch prayer led up to the event. This level of intra-church prayer was unprecedented. Young and old from all the churches came to pray for the unsaved and for the Lord's presence at "E2K." In reality, this city-wide altar of intercession was the foundation on which our gathering was built.

On Easter morning, the coliseum was filled with over ten thousand souls. The worship pastor from the Assembly of God church led a contemporary praise team. The Conservative Baptist minister of music directed a choir of more than two hundred. The pastor of an independent charismatic church got the enthusiastic nod from local pastors to present the gospel. It was clear our endeavor was well supported by the pillar of evangelistic responsibility to share Jesus with others.

Josue, a local Hispanic pastor, opened with an enthusiastic invocation in Spanish. Pam, a black gospel soloist, belted out "Amazing Grace," bringing the crowd to its feet. A team of talented children's workers from different churches worked together to create "Celebration Town" in an adjacent facility. Packets with coloring books, snack, and drink were prepared for children who sat through the service with their parents. A nursery was set up in the athletic training rooms in the coliseum. Indeed, this was a clear, visible expression of "the whole church, presenting the whole gospel, to the whole city."

Expenses for "E2K" were fully covered going in, and the Christians in attendance gave $60,000 to sow mercy into our city in two ways: to help build a new local homeless shelter, and provide primary funding for a school district summer program for at-risk kids. We presented the checks to city officials and school board administrators at the Courthouse on the National Day of Prayer. They were clearly overwhelmed, not just with the monetary gift, but by the fact that this was given on Easter Sunday by twenty-eight local congregations. As a part of our long range Vision Path, we are continuing to mobilize people in our churches to partner creatively with local schools by serving as tutors, lunch buddies for troubled students, and volunteer grounds crews. In the face of recent school budget cuts, our willingness to serve is finding a warm response. We've also put in place "LOVE, Inc." ("In the Name of Christ," originated by World Vision), a formal ministry of the CitiChurch of Corvallis designed to mobilize personnel and resources to meet local human needs. The pillar of a "no strings" compassion is imperative in any city-wide movement— a sensitive and sacrificial commitment to express our Lord's heart for the poor and underprivileged.

The highlight of E2K was watching both believers and unbelievers streaming in an hour before start time. We were seeing a living example of sacrificial unity that lifts up Jesus as the Risen King and offers his compassion to needy people. Many shared a sense of the pleasure and glory of the Lord settling in over the place. That night, from Portland to Salem to Eugene, the television reporting was positive and enthusiastic. Many of the reporters shared a common impression, "I've never seen anything like this!" Hear again the heartbeat of Jesus' prayer: "... one ... so that the world may believe" (Jn 17:21).

In the afterglow, I had an encounter in the local athletic

club Monday afternoon. A stockbroker friend from Salomon Smith Barney approached me, "That was incredible!" I didn't know at first what he was talking about. He went on. "I've never seen so many people from different churches in one place. It was the talk of the whole office this morning."

After the Easter 2000 gathering, we encountered the typical energy letdown from a big event. When people inquired, "Are you going to do this again next year?" we jokingly replied, "No, but we're forming an exploratory committee for "E3K" (Easter 3000!). Even after such a unifying event we continue to grapple with the hard questions: are we as leaders really growing in our personal prayer lives? How committed are our congregations to this ongoing vision to build a "house of prayer" in the city? Lord, what does commitment really look like over the long haul?

So, did God's glory pour out all over Corvallis? Well, yes and no. Yes, by touching his presence together as one people, in one place. Yes, by touching the needy of our city, and opening fresh favor with the city government and the school district. Yes, because we were obedient to a heavenly vision to keep meeting the needs of the poor and underprivileged. But no, we're also not yet seeing significant, ongoing spiritual breakthrough. Honestly, between the fall of 2000 and the time of this writing in the spring of 2001, we hit a classic plateau. In the aftermath of victory, the enemy has roamed our city as a roaring, angry lion, and we've had our share of discouragement, warfare, and turmoil in several key churches. So we continue to pray and obey, pressing through the plateaus. By summer 2001, our leadership team was back on track, working the "God-sized goals" of our long-term vision (see appendix 8).

Here's the perspective: long-term intercessory investment has been made. I've seen through the years that after cycles and seasons like this, the Spirit breathes on our brokenness, renews our desperation, and rekindles momentum.

So, wise, persevering leaders lay "tracks" of enduring biblical vision that keep right on going through the highs and lows, the praise gatherings, the outreaches, the death or departure of key leaders, and the seasonal strengths or weaknesses of local churches. Maintaining regularity, frequency, and fervency in vision-oriented prayer must be at the heart of all we do, or we'll all too quickly find ourselves moving "off the tracks."

Bringing the Blueprints to Life

It is a privilege to share with you this significant piece of my spiritual journey. In my city, and in all the other places I have mentioned, we continue to build on the four pillars of a city-wide movement, with our eyes fixed on Jesus. I want to encourage you to seek the Lord for what his unique blueprints are for your area. You may already be "down the road" with a city-wide movement. Or you may be just beginning to dream about what is on God's heart for your city.

There are no limitations. Nothing is impossible in the mysterious mix of our faith and his favor. There are no "cookie cutters," only clear biblical principles, and a lot of faith and perseverance. The rewards of choosing to walk in biblical unity are well worth it. I believe we're still in the early stages of an ongoing movement that will only gain in momentum.

I trust these pages have stirred you to break through barriers of unbelief, and press into new ground. But don't stop here. The appendix that follows provides a wealth of practical nuggets you may use to build the house of the Lord where you live, dwell, and dream.

In November 1997, I was invited to preach at King of Kings Assembly, a thriving congregation of assorted Jewish and Gentile Christians that meets at the YMCA in Jerusalem. The next day, a handful of leaders from assorted congregations gathered in Haifa for a prayer retreat, an annual gathering that has since come to be called "Men Meeting with God." The Holy Spirit impressed on me Paul's prayer for unity in the midst of the radical diversity of the emerging body of Christ, the "one new man" of Jews and Gentiles united in the all-inclusive love of Yeshua. Could Paul have asked God to hear and answer this bold prayer if it were not a realistic possibility? As I prayed for the leaders of that city, a place that stirs God's passion, I pray this for you, and for your city, to the ultimate praise and glory of our Lord's great name:

> May the God who gives endurance and encouragement give you a spirit of unity among yourselves as you follow Christ Jesus, so that with one heart and mouth you may glorify the God and Father of our Lord Jesus Christ. Accept one another, then, just as Christ accepted you, in order to bring praise to God.
>
> ROMANS 15:5-7

APPENDICES

PRACTICAL HELPS FOR DEVELOPING
CITY-WIDE PRAYER MOVEMENTS

What follows are some practical helps that may be relevant to your journey. Pastors, evangelists, para-church leaders, intercessors, key influencers from the business community, all should have a keen interest in the healthy growth of a prayer movement in a city. These are ideas, examples of things that have worked well. Some of the materials I have produced; others are credited. If any or all of this inspires you, take it, adapt it, contextualize it. Remember, there are principles and patterns for what the Spirit of God is doing in our day, but no "kingdom cookie cutters." And remember as well, this is all so new that all of us are still on a major learning curve. While we can discover and attempt to systematize both principles and practice, our primary source of advice is Jesus himself.

APPENDIX 1:
Calling Leaders to Prayer

Frontline Ministries
Frontline Ministries offers two or three-day leadership prayer retreat formats that balance waiting on God (personal renewal) with watching for the unfolding of Spirit-breathed strategies to impact a city (vision). In additon, Frontline offers leadership training, vision-casting events, city-reaching consultations for "city church" servant leaders, and speaking for city-wide gathersings.

Tom White also is an active Associate of International Renewal Ministries (IRM) and serves as a facilitator for Pastors Prayer Summits in the United States and overseas.

Frontline Ministries
P.O. Box 786
Corvallis OR 97339
541-754-1345
www.flministries.org (website)
tomwhite07@compuserve.com

Pastors Prayer Summits
IRM, founders and developers of the Pastors Prayer Summit model, offers
the original Pastors Prayer Summit which berings unity and a sustainable
movement of prayer among leaders in a city or regional context.

International Renewal Ministries
8435 NE Glisan St.
Portland, OR 97220
503-251-6455
irm@multnomah.edu

Prayer Summits in Australia, New Zealand, and Southeast Asia
Colin Shaw, resident of Toowoomba, Australia and an international
Associate of IRM, has launched Prayer Summits in Australia, New Zealand,
the Philippines, Papua New Guinea and India. Colin may be contacted
directly for Prayer Summits, vision-casting, and consultation in this region.

Colin Shaw
Toowoomba City Church
P.O. Box 2216
Toowoomba, Queensland 4350
AUSTRALIA
(07) 4638-2399
colinshaw@tcchurch.com.au

The Meaning and Purpose of a Prayer Summit
A Prayer Summit is defined as "a prolonged (typically four-day) life-changing
worship experience attended by a diversity of Christian leaders from specific,
geographical communities whose sole purpose is to seek God, his kingdom,
and his righteousness with the expectation that he will create and guide them
through a humbling, healing, uniting process that will lead them to a unity of
heart, mind, and mission and will qualify them for the blessing of God."

Our Mission
Our mission is to serve as a catalyst for unity in the body of Christ through
enriching and equipping activities for the leadership of the Church that will lead
to spiritual renewal, an increased spiritual harvest, and a change in society.

Values We Have in Common

- Above all, we value an ongoing, growing, personal relationship with Jesus Christ;
- We value the Bible as the Word of God, our final authority of faith and practice;
- We value a move of God initiated and sustained in as many geographic areas as possible;
- We value Christ-like leadership characterized by humility, brokenness, a servant's spirit and evidenced by transparency, openness, and vulnerability;
- We value the unity (not the uniformity) and health of the whole body of Christ;
- We value the ministry and therefore the support of local pastors and congregations;
- We value all members of the body of Christ regardless of their race, culture, gender, generation, or gifting;
- We value the importance of repentance and reconciliation being evident among church leaders and the entire body of Christ;
- We value relationships which transcend organizational structure;
- We value remaining totally submissive to the Holy Spirit at all times and in all decision making, respecting at all times the uniqueness and validity of what God is doing from place to place, culture to culture, and people to people;
- We value giving God all the glory with no self-promotion or self-seeking;
- We value a long-term sustainable movement more than isolated events;
- We value healthy, cooperative relationships with any and all ministries who are seeking to see a greater move of God initiated and sustained;
- We value the relational nature of prayer (with whom, for whom, and to whom we pray), not only the functional nature of prayer;
- We value the identification, establishment, and development of a local leadership team to carry the responsibilities of stewarding the vision and shepherding the prayer movement in a local community;
- We value personal and corporate renewal (revival) ... evangelism and ultimately... the transformation of society.

APPENDIX 2:
Mission Marin
Marin County, California
Agreement to Walk Together

"Do two walk together unless they have agreed to do so?"

AMOS 3:3

Mission Marin is a group of believers in the Lord Jesus Christ who recognize one another as God's larger church in Marin County. Its core group are the ministering leaders of participating local congregations who have agreed to walk together according to this document. Our core group agrees:

To embrace this mission: "Engaging the whole church in a passionate pursuit of God and a genuine expression of the gospel of Jesus Christ, in order to transform every sphere of life in Marin."

To submit to this vision: "To see a wide community of Christian believers in Marin uniting in prayer, walking in love and holiness, serving with compassion, sharing the gospel, and equipping one another."

To accept the following statements as our common core values:
1) Dependence upon God (Jn 15:4)
2) Trans-denominational, interdependent leadership   (1 Cor 3:4-6; Col 3:12)
3) One body, many congregations (Eph 4:1-6)
4) Every member equipped (Eph 4:11-13)
5) A heart for the lost (Mt 28:19-20)
6) Wholeheartedness (Col 3:23)

Because genuine participation is functional, not just theoretical, we also agree (allowing for God-directed exceptions):

- To meet weekly together in prayer to build relationship and trust.
- To attend annually the Mission Marin Prayer Summit to hear from God together.

- To fellowship monthly at the Mission Marin Luncheon, as a gathering point for new participants and a forum for mutual encouragement and communication.
- To support, encourage, promote, and participate in Mission Marin county-wide events at least two times each year, to spread the vision and blessing to our congregations.

Because our relationships are based on our spiritual unity in Christ, we commit to value and validate the unique callings of each minister and each local church and to pursue reconciliation and peace, wherever possible. Therefore, we also agree:

- To seek opportunities from the Lord to minister together/exchange pulpits and gather our people together for times of worship, prayer, and fellowship.
- To deal redemptively with one another in love, according to the biblical principles of restoration (Mt 18, Gal 6), to avoid factions and divisiveness.
- To pray for and bless one another's ministry, privately and publicly, and not to discredit or undermine one another's mission by attitude, word, or deed.
- To pursue dialogue when conflicts arise, according to biblical guidelines.
- Not to receive or foster resentment, gossip, or careless accusation against one another, but to encourage resolution among the involved parties.
- Not to practice "sheep stealing" nor to receive church transfers without contact and counsel with their former pastor, yet to support and bless those whom the Holy Spirit may lead to another congregation.

When seeking to apply the above processes to a specific situation, we will direct any question or difference that arises to the Servant Leader Team, who will appoint a three-pastor team to review the matter and give counsel. If that proves unsatisfactory, we may also seek counsel from ministers outside of our county. Any question as to the application of the above processes to a specific situation may be directed to the Servant-Leader Team, who will appoint a three-pastor team to review the matter and give counsel.

Because God-appointed leadership is vital to the progress of his work, we also agree:

- To recognize and encourage servant leaders of Mission Marin, whom God raises up to give an extra measure of time and energy to the cause of Christ through Mission Marin.

Finally, we submit one to another, in mutual accountability, for the above agreements. We realize that this accountability will be guided by the New Covenant of Christ's love and grace and will be based on the Biblical principles of Matthew 18:1-20, Galatians 6:1, 1 Timothy 5:19, and Hebrews 10:24-25.

And we may know that by entering into this agreement to walk together in unity we will benefit in the following ways:

1) We will be prayed for regularly by one another.
2) We will be respected and appreciated by one another.
3) We will be encouraged to share our burdens with one another.
4) We will receive good counsel and courage from one another.
5) We will share in the excitement of God's greater work in Marin.
6) We will be joined by one another in the battles we face.

This agreement is renewable annually.

I AGREE, signed _____Date _____

APPENDIX 3

Role and Qualifications Description
For a City Church Servant Leader

Committed, competent leadership is required to steward the emerging vision of "One Church, many congregations." A servant leader (or "city facilitator") is neither elected or self-appointed, but selected by God, then recognized and affirmed by colleagues. Servant Leaders are typically selected and commissioned at a Prayer Summit or leaders' prayer retreat for a one year renewable term. Additional servant leaders may be brought on and confirmed at the discretion of the existing team, as led by the Holy Spirit.

Qualifications:
1. A servant leader must exhibit qualities consistent with standards for elders outlined in Titus and 1 Timothy. Maturity, longevity of ministry, breadth of esteem, and realistic availability of time also must be considered. A passion for building the City Church must burn strongly in the heart of the servant leader.
2. A servant leader must exhibit a passion to grow in his own personal prayer life, and be accountable to fellow leaders for this growth.
3. A servant leader must carry the vision of one Body, one Spirit, one faith, have a passion for building up the city-wide Body, and steward the mission to mobilize the whole Body to reach the whole city with the whole gospel.
4. A servant leader must exhibit a high level of ownership of and commitment to the city church vision, and have a realistic availability of time and energy to commit to:

- a minimum of one servant leader meeting per month
- two overnight or day-long prayer/planning retreats each year
- participation in pastoral and Body-wide prayer meetings

Chief responsibilities of a servant leader team include:

- Seeking the Lord earnestly for his vision for how to walk together in obeying Jesus' Great Commandment and the Great Commission.
- Planning and coordinating an annual Prayer Summit or Leaders' Retreat.
- Overseeing the Pastors' Prayer Group(s) in the area.
- Overseeing and communicating with the intercessors: Meeting with the intercessory team at least two times each year for worship, prayer, and building relationships.
- Overseeing and guiding the demographic and spiritual mapping teams.
- Coordinating a master calendar of prayer, training, and conference events to minimize scheduling conflicts.
- Calling the wider Body to gather for united worship and prayer, as led by the Spirit.

As issues occur in individual congregations in the city, the servant leader team may be asked to come alongside and help resolve conflict, as invited by a board or denominational overseer. If pastoral peers fall prey to sin, servant leaders may exercise their moral influence in calling a colleague to repentance, reconciliation, and restitution.

As issues arise in the movement (theological, style of prayer or worship, personality tensions, etc.), servant leaders will continually seek God for the grace and wisdom to maintain the unity of the Spirit in the bond of peace.

APPENDIX 4

Church of Marin
County-Wide Prayer Team
Covenant and Requirements for Membership
(provided by Deb Roy, Marin County, California)

What follows are the guidelines for intercessors wishing to participate in praying on the county-wide Prayer Team. We recognize that as we grow together as a team and come to better understand and love each other, these guidelines may need to be altered.

As a Church of Marin prayer support team member, I agree to abide by the following commitments during my tenure on the team:

Spiritual Responsibilities:
1. I have accepted Jesus Christ as my Lord and Savior, and am committed to developing an ongoing and vital relationship with him.
2. I am in submission to a pastor in my local church body and I commit to developing ongoing relationships somewhere where I am held accountable along with other believers.

Team Responsibilities:
1. I agree to hold prayer requests in the strictest confidence. I understand that anything shared or prayed in the meeting is covered by this agreement. I agree to share and discuss requests only with people on the prayer team. I understand that violation of this confidentiality violates the trust of the pastors of the county and of the team, and that I may be asked to step down from the team if I violate this responsibility.
2. I understand that my presence on the team is an important part of intercession for the county. I agree to attend and participate in as many of the prayer team meetings as possible. I agree to take prayer requests for times when I miss the meetings, unless unforeseen circumstances prevent my participation. The requests will be mailed to my home or communicated via telephone (preferably in person, messages will be left only if you live alone), or via private email.

3. I agree to pray as the Holy Spirit instructs me throughout the course of the week. I agree to stand as a watchman for the county as the Lord leads. If urgent words from the Lord or concerns come to me in prayer, I will relay these to one of the Intercessor Servant Leader Team (ISLT) members.

4. I agree to refrain from communication with pastors in regard to their prayer requests in public places or during times they are ministering (such as Sunday mornings, family groups, county-wide gatherings, etc.). It is, of course, okay to discuss needs if the pastor initiates the discussion during these times. (Please also refer to the section on prophetic words, in the Responsible Handling of Spiritual Gifts section).

5. I agree to accept loving correction by the Pastor Servant Leader Team (PSLT) pastors, my own pastor, or the ISLT in the event it becomes necessary.

Responsible Handling of Spiritual Gifts

It is hoped that the fullness of all of the gifts of the Spirit will be expressed through the intercessors serving the county. (1 Cor 12 and 1 Cor 14:39-40) It is expected that intercessors will come from different traditions within the body of Christ and that all of the gifts are valuable to the process of praying for the county and for the lost. It is assumed that we are all growing in the gifts and need a safe place to exercise these gifts to build up and encourage the Body. To that end, the use of all of the gifts will be encouraged. As the maintenance of order is important in any gathering, I agree to adhere to the following standards of conduct:

The gift of tongues: If I am blessed with the gift of tongues, I agree to use it openly only when someone gifted in interpretation is present (1 Cor 14:26-28). I also understand that I may pray out in a tongue if directed by the Holy Spirit, all the while praying that I will receive the interpretation of the message (1 Cor 14:13). Other than these times, I understand that I am welcome to pray very quietly in tongues in such a manner as not to distract or disrupt the flow of intercession in the meeting.

The gift of prophecy: In time, it is expected that God will speak to and through the intercessors in a prophetic way. The gifting of the prophet is understood quite differently in various Christian traditions. While not an essential of the faith, scripture says prophecy is to be desired as a gifting and that it is not to be despised. With this viewpoint in mind, I agree to the following guidelines for delivering a word or impression from the Lord:

1. I will ask the Lord if this word is for public consideration at this particular public meeting, or if it should be kept within my private prayer closet.
2. If the Lord indicates it should be publicly shared, quickly jot it down and hand it to the nearest ISLT member. They will review the word and try to discern, with the Lord's help, the best time to share the word so that it enhances the flow of intercession and workings of the Spirit within the meeting.
3. If the ISLT feels the word should be kept quiet and shared privately, they'll let intercessors know and will spend time with him or her at the conclusion of the meeting. The intercessor should wait until that time to further discuss the word (1 Cor 14:29-33).

Words (prophetic or encouraging) received in private prayer: Many pastors are unfamiliar with the giving and receiving of prophetic words as understood in charismatic and pentecostal traditions and therefore may not openly receive "words" offered by intercessors. In respect of the varying traditions regarding prophecy within Marin County I agree that:

1. Nothing written will be submitted to any pastor in the county without first submitting it to the ISLT. The exception to this is your own pastor, and then "words" should be submitted within your own style and tradition. If the "word" you receive is for the county or you feel it applies to the Church of Marin, it must be submitted to the ISLT before submitting it to *any* pastor. The ISLT will contact you as soon as possible to let you know if it's okay to pass along your word.
2. I also agree to refrain from telephone calls, e-mails, or any other communication form of prophetic words until cleared by the ISLT.

Relational Responsibilities: (Mt 18:15-17) As we grow in our gifts and learn to work together, disagreements or offenses may occur. None of us will always hear God perfectly as we pray or we may pray out of our own human promptings. In these times, grace will need to be given. Remember that Jesus came first full of grace and then full of truth! Knowing that a balance of both grace and truth is essential in all relationships, and in a spirit of humility, unity, and love, I agree to the following relational guidelines:

1. If offended, I will ask God to help me and to provide wisdom— agreeing to keep the matter private and in my own prayer closet until the Lord releases me to speak to the person in love. The only exception to this will be a prompting by the Lord to approach the person in private as soon as the meeting is over.
2. If after privately praying, I am still troubled, and the offense is still present or reoccurs, I agree to follow the steps outlined in Matthew 18:15-17:

a. I will go to the person privately to discuss my concern and seek reconciliation of the relationship.
b. If the person is unresponsive to my concern, and I still feel a need to discuss it, I will approach the ISLT, who will do their best to assist me. If they are in agreement with my concern, or sense the need for reconciliation in the relationship, they will set up a meeting between myself and the other person, for the purpose of bringing understanding and resolution.
c. If the person is unresponsive, or the offensive behavior continues, the matter will be submitted to the Pastor's Servant Leader Team (PSLT). All concerned parties will meet and the pastors will determine the best course of action. At this point I agree to abide by the judgment and decision of the PSLT.

I have read and understand the above guidelines for participating on the Church of Marin Prayer Team. I am in agreement with these guidelines, except as noted in writing:

Signed: _____

_____

Date: _____

I understand that the intercessor named in this covenant will be participating in "Church of Marin" county-wide prayer. This person is in good standing in our congregation and is in appropriate submission to the spiritual authority in our church. He/she has my blessing to participate.

Pastor's Signature:_____

Date: _____

APPENDIX 5:
City-Wide United Prayer Gatherings
Suggested Formats

These formats have been used extensively and successfully in numerous contexts. A city leadership team should evaluate every gathering, and make changes as needed to improve future events. Even with such formats, it is always good to remain open to the on-site leadings of the Holy Spirit.

In most cases, worship flows best with an established worship team from one congregation. Other instrumentalists and vocalists may be added. A listening/facilitating team of three leaders works the best to gauge the pace of the gathering and discern how the Lord may want to lead.

Two-Hour Format
"The Church Together"

5:50 *Worship Warm-up, Ingathering.*

6:00 *Welcome.* Psalm 133:1-3 (or other Psalm) on screen for corporate recitation. Brief invocation.

6:05 *Praise and Adoration.* Start celebrative, move toward intimate and reflective. (Option: mid-set, pre-assign three people at stage or floor mikes, 30 seconds each, to extol the Lord from the Word or in prayer.)

6:45 *Giving Thanks.* Three or four men or women express thanks for something concrete God has done.

6:50 *Bringing the Word.* (Keep this brief. Suggest 12–15 minutes maximum. This can be a word on repentance, unity, prayer, vision, faith, etc. This needs to lead into and inspire prayer.)

7:05 *Prayer Segment #1.* With John 17:21-23 or Ephesians 4:1-3 on screen, have four pastors and/or intercessors pray for increased unity, breaking of walls, resolution of local issues, etc. Finish the segment with a familiar chorus (seamless), using light synthesizer or acoustic guitar.

7:15 *Prayer Segment #2.* With Colossians 4:2 on screen, have folks form huddles of 7-8 and ask the Lord to stir an increase of hunger for prayer in the Body. Clarify that no one is obligated to pray. Some are socially uncomfortable with pressure to participate. It's all right to "amen" others in agreement. Finish this segment with a transition chorus (facilitator cues worship leader).

7:25 *Prayer Segment #3.* Pray for a local issue. Have someone give a 2–3 minute briefing, e.g., local schools, government concerns, social issues. Option A: Pre-arrange people to pray at mikes. Option B: open mikes, ask those who feel led to pray line up, 3–4 at each of two mikes, and pray, 2 minutes maximum.

7:35 *Transition chorus.*

7:40 *Announcements and Offering.* Upcoming events (on screen also), and offering.

7:50 *Praise Wrap.* Lead in from the offering using celebrative music.

8:00 *Blessing and Benediction.*

90-Minute Format
"Pursuing His Presence, Praying His Heart"

5:50 *Worship Warm-Up.*

6:00 *Welcome and Opening Prayer.*

6:05 *Praise and Adoration.*

6:30 *Prayer.* Pastor or intercessor gives thanks for what God is doing in the city.

6:35 *Biblical focus* on seeking the Lord.(e.g., Ps 27, 84; Lam 3:17-40)

6:45 *Prayer Segment #1:* Setting Our Hearts to Seek the Lord. Ask people to enter into prayer individually or with a friend or spouse. Allow a few minutes to reflect on the Scripture and the challenge, and re-commit to seek the Lord. Then, have 3 pre-assigned pray-ers offer prayer at the microphone. Confessing and repenting of spiritual lukewarmness and busy-ness may be appropriate here. Transition: worship team eases in with a familiar chorus.

6:55 *Prayer Segment #2.* Option A: Repentance: If the Holy Spirit is bringing conviction, invite people to pray alone, with a friend, or come forward to the altar. Worship team leads in quiet, reflective worship. Option B: Bearing One Another's Burdens. Read Galatians 6:2, Hebrews 4:12-16, and James 5:13, move people into huddles of 6–8, ask them to go around the circle and succinctly share any burdens or concerns, then go back around and pray, with Hebrews 4 as a guide. Transition chorus (worship team or solo keyboard or acoustic guitar)

7:10 *Prayer Segment #3.* Prayer for the pastors and their churches. Ask pastors, associates, and spouses to come forward, then ask others to "wrap" around them. Either prearrange several to pray, or pass a hand-held microphone to those burdened to pray for the churches; emphasis may be on increased hunger for prayer, protection, empowerment of ministries, courage to lead, etc. Transition chorus. ("Bind Us Together," "Shield About Me," etc.)

7:20 *Announcements and Offering.*

7:25 *Praise Wrap.*

7:30 *Benediction.*

APPENDIX 6:
Gatekeepers and Watchmen
Walking Together

In developing city-wide prayer movements, we are stepping onto new turf. I want to share some seasoned thoughts about pastors and intercessors walking and working together. This is not an easy area. Both have very different callings and "filters" by which they discern what God is saying and what to do with what he is saying. It's a lot of work for these two to "get inside one another's heads." Endless misunderstanding and awkwardness seem to arise between them regularly.

I believe the Lord wants to weave the valuable functions of leadership and intercession together to release his vision, empowered by the breath of the Spirit. I commend to you a book by Eddie and Alice Smith that offers wisdom on this matter: *Intercessors and Pastors: The Emerging Partnership of Watchmen and Gatekeepers.*

God has given to his church the offices of apostle, prophet, evangelist, pastor, and teacher for the building of the body of Christ. It is not clear from Scripture, however, that intercession is an office in the Church. It cannot be documented from Scripture that it is anywhere acknowledged as a distinct gift of the Spirit. Rather, intercessory prayer is something in which all believers can engage. (See Rom 8:26, 27; 1 Tm 2:1-8; Hb 4:14-16). Thus, I can be a pastor, a teacher, an exhorter, a healer, or an administrative leader, and enter into "intercessory prayer" that connects a desperate need on earth to the unlimited resources of heaven. You can possess any gift or gifts of God's Spirit, hold an appointed office or not hold an office, and flow in intercessory prayer as the Spirit guides you.

I am nevertheless convinced that, though not an office or special gifting, men and women indeed are called into ministries of intercession where their primary focus and function is faithful, fervent prayer. I continue to meet people who are clearly "called to the wall" of a city or region (Is 62:6). A man or woman may be endowed with mercy, discernment, faith, even helps or leadership, yet be led by the Lord to exercise those gifts through a ministry of prayer.

And among those that are so called, I believe there is a distinction between those who give themselves to fervent intercession on a regular basis, and those who do it occasionally. I would describe the first category as "intercessors." I would describe the second category as "prayer warriors," men and women who come out for prayer meetings, carry prayer burdens, and pray with commitment and passion, but not as their primary ministry.

Many pastors have grown to be suspicious and afraid of aggressive intercessors who may bring them "words, warnings, and visions." They just don't know what to do with them. And intercessors often feel misunderstood and disenfranchised by pastoral leadership, feeling tolerated at best.

Dangers of sin and wrong attitude exist on both sides of this equation. Intercessors must guard against pride ("I see what God is doing, and the pastor doesn't"), rebellion ("if he doesn't get this and go with it, I will!"), judgment ("he just doesn't know the things of the Spirit"), bitterness (letting the pain of rejection settle into your soul), and negativity (seeing the cup always "half empty" rather than "half full"). If an intercessory group is largely female (which is common), the participants must be aware of their own unresolved emotional issues that may be triggered by a largely male authority group.

At the same time, male pastors must also be honest about our issues of pride, control, and anger, and be accountable for them. In many cases, we do not lead with sensitivity and love. Rather, we operate out of a self-protective mode that serves to perpetuate male dominance and further aggravate wounds our sisters are carrying.

Discerning and resolving these kinds of problems requires great understanding and patience.

With patience and perseverance, leaders should take initiative to affirm and bless those called to the ministry of intercession, to draw them in, and to turn them loose to pray. Maintain clear lines of communication between the pastoral leaders and those called to the ministry of intercession. God can surely mesh these two ministries together at the local church level and in the city environment.

APPENDIX 7:
Perspectives on Diagnostic Research

With the increased activity of city-wide movements has come a keen interest in what was known initially as "spiritual mapping." The book, *The Last of the Giants* (1994), made author George Otis, Jr. the chief pioneer and architect of the discipline of strategic discernment. His work and writings have defined the standards of diagnostic research, most recently with the publication of *Informed Intercession*. It is not my purpose here to re-articulate the essence of George's work. Instead I would like to affirm the role of spiritual research in the development of a city movement and to offer a few observations. Beyond this, I refer readers to the two videos produced by The Sentinel Group, *Transformations* and *Transformations II*.

George suggests that we approach a community or region with three questions: What is wrong here, how did things get this way, and what do saints in the present do to change it? When he says "wrong," he refers to matters of spiritual deception and bondage, socioeconomic injustice, pervasive ungodliness, aspects of a culture that are contrary to the character of Jesus Christ and the rule of his kingdom.

To bring this down to the bottom shelf, let's say your city is plagued by an above-average occurrence of divorce and domestic violence. You ask the question, "What really ails this place?" Are there spiritual or cultural roots that would offer some clues as to why things are the way they are in the present?

Spiritual research can trace the following: (1) the identity of the earliest settlers of the land and the nature of any rebellion against God and subsequent allegiances with demonic deities; (2) occurrences of racial or social injustice, when certain people abused and dominated other people; (3) instances of severe cultural trauma such as wars, massacres, or natural catastrophes.

The pursuit of spiritual diagnostic research is a discipline that illumines the dark corners of a city or nation's history and informs what we pray about, and how. It can provide the substance for the Lord's call to "turn from our wicked ways." What, precisely, are the wicked ways of the inhabitants of Corvallis, Oregon, of San Francisco, California, or of Tuscaloosa, Alabama? Our sincere prayer might be: "Show us where our ways have conflicted with your ways."

One of the goals of the research is to produce an actual time line of the major events that have shaped a city's spiritual history. This information is to be used primarily to compel believers to respond with repentance for sins of the past (see Neh 9 and Dn 9), to help promote reconciliation to groups that have been offended and disenfranchised, and to inform and guide the intercessory prayers of saints as they pray, "Thy kingdom come, thy will be done" here, in this place, at this time.

Often I encounter people who ask, "Can't we just seek the Lord, repent of our sins, pray together, and ask him to bring an awakening to our city? Do we really have to do all this work, dig up all the garbage, and drag out our skeletons before God will bless us?" In my view, the Lord can surely enable a group of people to humble themselves and embrace a repenting of the past sins of forefathers (see Dn 9 and Ezr 9) without tediously exposing all the muck of the past and legalistically endeavoring to right every wrong. But it is also good wisdom to ask the honest question, "Lord, are there altars of offense in our history that still grieve you, and hinder your favor?" We also need to guard againts a mindset that says, "if we get all our ducks in a row, then God will bless us." We'll never get all of our issues fully worked out.

Let's understand that when we seek, in humility and sincerity, to make right those things we or our forefathers have done wrong, we appeal to the Lord's mercy and pray that he will shower fresh favor upon us.

In my city, one of our researchers provided a simple analysis of the stronghold of humanism in Corvallis. At one of our weekly times of intercession, the pastors, as the "elders in the gates" of the city, intentionally renounced the roots of humanistic attitudes, and invited God to further establish his lordship over our lives. Observational data moved us toward informed, productive prayer. It also sharpened our ability to recognize the power of humanism on an ongoing basis.

If such spiritual research points us in the direction of true repentance and restoration of covenantal relationship with God and with one another, it has helped us, regardless of whether we define it as a formal discipline or as simple common sense.

In the context of the leadership infrastructure in a city-wide movement, I believe that the researchers must maintain an intentional commitment to pastors and leaders, being open to their correction and guided by their counsel. Often researchers already are serving as watchmen on the walls, carrying a burden to see the redemptive destiny of a city come to fruition. The right people, endowed with both the character and competence to take this research forward, will have the tenacity required to see such projects through to completion.

APPENDIX 8:
Defining the Mission, Vision, Values, and Goals of a "Citi-Church"

Several years back I spent time with a small group of leaders who were seeking the Lord for understanding on the development of city-wide prayer movements. That meeting provided the impetus and personnel for what is now CitiReach, International. At this gathering, Jim Herrington of Houston and Jarod Roth, now the U.S. Director for the Foursquare denomination, led us through a "VisionPath" exercise, a simple but extremely helpful process of defining a group's mission, vision, values, and goals. About this same time, my own city of Corvallis was beginning to chart its own course, finding its identity and mandate as a "CitiChurch."

Soon after, I called our team together to spend a day producing a VisionPath. We locked ourselves in a room at Oregon State University and labored for fourteen hours. We mixed our deliberations with prayer and worship, opening ourselves to the leading of the Holy Spirit.

I would like to provide here a simple model of what a typical VisionPath might look like. You can also find one that is more defined and more detailed by looking over the shoulders of the movements in Spokane, Washington (www.missionspokane.org) and Mission Houston (www.missionhouston.org). These cities have aggressively defined goals and key leverage actions with specific personnel and date assignments for each goal.

CitiChurch of Corvallis

Our Mission
To engage the whole church of Corvallis to disciple the whole city with the Gospel of Jesus Christ.

Our Vision

To be a praying, united community of Jesus' disciples walking together in love, to demonstrate the reality of our oneness in Christ, "so that the world may believe" (Jn 17:17-23)

Our Values

- *One Church of the city expressed in diverse congregations*
- *Devotion to prayer and worship (personal & corporate)*
- *Submission to the Lordship of Jesus Christ & the authority of the Bible*
- *A heart to reach the lost*
- *Value, respect & support of one another*
- *Utter dependence upon God*

Our God-Sized Goals

God-Sized Goal #1: UNITY

On an ongoing basis, to embrace, maintain, demonstrate and celebrate our oneness in the love of Jesus Christ (Jn 17:17-23; Eph 4:1-3; Rom 15:1-13).

God-Sized Goal #2: PRAYER

To be an effectively functioning prayer community in the hearts of individual believers, within and among the congregations of our city (Col 4:2; 1 Tm 2:1-8).

God-Sized Goal #3: CHURCHES BLESSING CHURCHES

To encourage a spirit of team ministry among Corvallis churches, cooperating and collaborating on ministry endeavors when and where possible.

God-Sized Goal #4: TOUCHING CORVALLIS WITH MERCY

To find practical ways to minister the grace and mercy of the Lord to the felt needs of people in our city.

God-Sized Goal #5: KINGDOM GROWTH

Increase church attendance in Corvallis evangelical churches from 10% to 15% of the population by the end of 2005, believing God for conversion growth through all forms of outreach, church planting, and personal witness.

This is our second "run" at determining God-sized goals for the city-wide church. It is encouraging to note that two of our initial goals set in the spring of 1998 (to increase the Church's relevance and viability and the public perception thereof, and to increase inter-church prayer and worship) were substantially met in the gathering together of over 85 percent of the churches of the city under one roof for a united celebration of Jesus' resurrection on Easter morning, 2000 (described in chapter eight).

We remind ourselves regularly not to make these goals ends in themselves. We're committed to revisit and evaluate them on an annual basis, being flexible to adjust and fine-tune them as we go forward on our journey. As we faithfully pursue God-given goals and saturate this pursuit with frequent and fervent prayer, the Lord can choose to pour out his presence into our midst at any time, and in any way.

APPENDIX 9
Websites For Strategic Prayer Mobilization

The following websites may serve as entry points for information helpful in the birthing and building of city-wide prayer movements.

National Networks

www.lighthousemovement.com	Lighthouse Movement
www.missionamerica.org	Mission America Coalition
www.NALCPL.net	National Association of Local Church Prayer Leaders
www.nppn.org	National Pastors Prayer Network
www.nationalprayer.org	National Prayer Committee
www.usprayertrack.org	U.S. Prayer Track

International Networks

www.openheaven.com	International Revival Network
www.24-7prayer.com 24-7	worldwide prayer movement

National Prayer Organizations

www.lighthousereport.com	Campus Crusade Lighthouses
www.citireach.org	CitiReach, International

www.ehc.org	Every Home for Christ
www.flministries.org	Frontline Ministries
www.globalharvest.org	Global Harvest Ministries
www.harvestevan.org	Harvest Evangelism
www.harvestprayer.com	Harvest Prayer Ministries
www.ifa-usapray.org	Intercessors for America
www.lydiafellowship.org	Lydia Fellowship
www.momsintouch.org	Moms in Touch
www.multnomah.edu	Pastors Prayer Summits
www.prayertransformation.org	Prayer Transformation Ministries
www.praymag.com	PRAY! Magazine
www.sentinelgroup.org	Sentinel Group
www.waymakers.org	Waymakers

City-Wide Prayer Movements

www.praychicago.org	Chicago, Illinois
www.churchofmodesto.com	The Church of Modesto
www.copgny.org	Concerts of Prayer, Greater New York
www.embraceomaha.com	Embrace Omaha
www.floridaprayer.org	Florida Prayer Network
www.missionfirstcoast.org	Greater Jacksonville, Florida
www.boston2001.net	Hearts for Boston / Boston 2001
www.missioncarolina.org	Mission Carolina
www.cleveland.org	Mission Cleveland
www.missionhouston.org	Mission Houston, Texas
www.praylubbock.com	Pray Lubbock
www.praytwincities.org	Pray Twin Cities
www.missionspokane.org	Spokane, Washington
www.missionmaine.org	Vision Maine

Statewide Prayer Networks

www.michiganspn.org	Michigan Strategic Prayer Network
www.prayernetoregon.org	PrayerNet Oregon
www.praytexas.com	Pray Texas

NOTES

Preface
A Script Rewritten

1. Hawthorne and Kendrick, *Prayerwalking* (Orlando, Fla.: Creation House, 1993).
2. Joe Aldrich, *Reunitas* (Sisters, Ore.: Multnomah, 1994).

ONE
My Heart, His Home

1. Underhill, Evelyn, *The House of the Soul* (London: Methuen, many editions), 116–19.
2. Tozer, A.W., *The Pursuit of God* (Camp Hill, Penn.: Christian Publications, 1982) 27.

TWO
A Call to the Construction Site

1. Aldrich, *Reunitas*.
2. Francis Frangipane, *The House of the Lord* (Lake Mary, Fla.: Creation House, 1991), 33.

FOUR
Giving Leadership to the City-Wide Church

1. Jim Herrington, Mike Bonem, and James Furr, *Leading Congregational Change* (San Francisco, Calif.: Jossey-Bass Publishers, 2000).

FIVE
The Bottom Line Is Love

1. Frangipane, *The House of the Lord.*
2. Larry Crabb, *The Safest Place on Earth* (Nashville, Tenn.: Word, 1999), 32.

SEVEN
Varieties of City-Wide Prayer

1. E.M. Bounds, *The Best of E.M. Bounds* (Grand Rapids, Mich.: Baker Books, 1981.